IMAGES
of America

Ss. Peter and
Paul Jesuit
Detroit's Oldest Church

Against the gleaming modern backdrop of Detroit's riverfront Renaissance Center is the sturdy outline of Ss. Peter and Paul Jesuit Church, its cornerstone laid in 1844. The Roman Catholic church is one of the oldest buildings in the city and the oldest worship structure of any denomination in Detroit. The church is in the photograph's center and its back side is defined by St. Catherine's Chapel, which now houses the Pope Francis Center to aid the homeless. Adjacent to the church, on the left, is the University of Detroit Mercy Law School. Across from the church are the University of Detroit Mercy Law School clinics, housed in a historic 19th-century fire engine house. (Photograph by Mary Schroeder.)

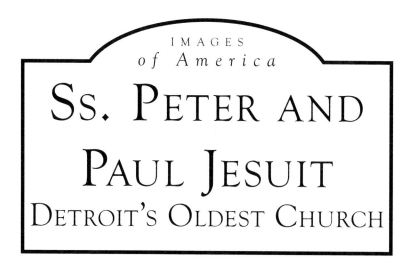

IMAGES
of America

Ss. Peter and Paul Jesuit
Detroit's Oldest Church

Patricia Montemurri

ARCADIA
PUBLISHING

Published by Arcadia Publishing
Charleston, South Carolina

Printed in the United States of America

Library of Congress Control Number: 2023935513

For all general information, please contact Arcadia Publishing:
Telephone 843-853-2070
Fax 843-853-0044
E-mail sales@arcadiapublishing.com
For customer service and orders:
Toll-Free 1-888-313-2665

Visit us on the Internet at www.arcadiapublishing.com

Much of what I love about Detroit starts at Ss. Peter and Paul Jesuit Church. This book is dedicated to the man I married at the church, Paul G. Diehl, educated by Jesuit priests and brothers in Detroit and Milwaukee and who taught for 36 years at the University of Detroit Jesuit High School and Academy.

CONTENTS

Acknowledgments   6

Introduction   7

1.   A Cathedral for Detroit   11

2.   A Jesuit Foundation   23

3.   The Parish School   35

4.   The Jesuit Imprint Grows   47

5.   Faith in Service   65

6.   Transitions   81

7.   Traditions   91

8.   The People of God Today   103

About the Organization   127

ACKNOWLEDGMENTS

When we married, my husband and I said our vows in the heart of Detroit. We were married at the oldest church in the city, Ss. Peter and Paul Jesuit, on one of the hottest days of 1989. We committed our love and lives to each other in a church that has shown a historic commitment to Detroit stretching over nearly two centuries.

This book would not be possible without the infinite patience of Lydia Maola, the parish's director of operations; the church's pastor, the Reverend Gary Wright, SJ; and parishioners Al Fields and Carol Goll.

Thank you to photographers Tom Hagerty, Diane Weiss, and longtime parishioner Mary Schroeder for their talent.

Thank you to the many archivists and researchers who accommodated my requests, including Patricia Higo of the University of Detroit Mercy; Veronica Buchanan of the Sisters of Charity of Cincinnati; Ann Knake of the Jesuit Archives & Research Center; Jennifer Meacham of the Sisters, Servants of the Immaculate Heart of Mary Archives; and Sister Carolyn Osiek, RSCJ, of the Society of the Sacred Heart. Thanks also to Ron Bernas of the University of Detroit Mercy; Sungae Kerschenheiter of the University of Detroit Mercy Law School; and Bonnie Leone, the author of an Arcadia Publishing book of a neighbor church, *Detroit's Holy Family Church: 100 Years of Sicilian Tradition*.

Thank you to Michael Stechschulte, the editor of the Archdiocese of Detroit website, the Detroit Catholic. Thanks to Jacob Yesh-Brochstein. Thank you to Elizabeth Clemens of the Walter P. Reuther Library, Archives of Labor and Urban Affairs, Wayne State University. Thanks to Thomas O'Keefe at University of Detroit Jesuit High School. Thank you to Debbie Miszak, who took many photographs of parish activities and members for this book.

The photographs in this book come from the Ss. Peter and Paul Jesuit Parish archives unless otherwise noted.

I much appreciate the patience and encouragement of my Arcadia Publishing title manager Caitrin Cunningham, senior production editor Ryan Vied, and Crystal Murray, front list manager. Thank you.

INTRODUCTION

When Cardinal Jorge Mario Bergoglio of Buenos Aires became pope in 2013, it was the first time that a priest from the Jesuit order was chosen to lead the universal Catholic Church. Under the papacy of Pope Francis, there has been a renewed focus on the contributions of Jesuit priests and brothers worldwide. In Michigan, the Jesuits have been a presence since European settlers first came to the New World.

Throughout the late 1660s, missionary priests from the Society of Jesus, the order's formal name, explored the Great Lakes. Michigan cities such as Marquette and Charlevoix are named after Jesuit explorers. The Jesuit Père Jacques Marquette established St. Ignace, named after the order's founder, St. Ignatius of Loyola, in the Upper Peninsula in 1671 as a Huron Native American Catholic community. When Antoine de la Mothe Cadillac founded the French settlement of Detroit in 1701, he was accompanied by two priests, including a Jesuit. The order served the indigenous Huron Catholic community in the Detroit area until 1781.

The Jesuits did not come back to Detroit until 1877, when the local Catholic bishop asked them to start a school aimed at furthering the education of Catholic teenaged boys and young men in the city. To commence their work, Bishop Caspar Borgess gave the Jesuits the keys to Detroit's Catholic cathedral—because he was building a new one. They became stewards of Ss. Peter and Paul Jesuit Church, built in 1848, stocky and orange-brick solid, on one of the city's prestigious thoroughfares, Jefferson Avenue.

Some 175 years after it was dedicated in 1848, Ss. Peter and Paul stands as the oldest church building of any denomination in Detroit. Detroit's oldest church is not an ornate, eye-catching showstopper. But its legacy of ministry and service deserves a spotlight.

The parish is the mother church for the Jesuits' remarkable impact in the Detroit area. The Jesuits who arrived in 1877 to take over stewardship of the church were committed to establishing Catholic education. The parish was at the center of Jesuit activities and educational outreach through the 1920s, when the Jesuits' footprint grew as the city did, with the establishment of the new University of Detroit and University of Detroit High School campuses in northwest Detroit. Traditions established at Ss. Peter and Paul continue to flourish, such as the Red Mass for lawyers, the first of which in the United States was held at the church in 1877 and continues to this day.

Its history is documented in precious leather-bound volumes in legible script from 175 years ago that record the first baptism in the church on January 2, 1849, of Frederick Henry Merritt and the first marriage at its altar of Catherine Reid and Dennis Dogherty on January 8, 1849.

Other Catholic parishes and Protestant congregations in Detroit date their establishment to the years before the construction of Ss. Peter and Paul. But none of them occupy a building older than the orange-brick structure at Jefferson Avenue and St. Antoine Street. The parish of Ste. Anne de Detroit, its founding dating to Detroit's settlement by Cadillac, occupied seven different structures before the current church was dedicated in 1887. Old St. Mary's Catholic Church, which anchors Detroit's Greektown, was founded in 1838, but its iconic current home was built in the mid-1880s.

Most Holy Trinity, the city's second-oldest Catholic parish, was founded in 1834 to serve English-speaking Catholics from Ireland. Shortly after Bishop Peter Paul Lefevere's cathedral, named to reflect his own patron saints, was dedicated in June 1848, he ordered Holy Trinity Church closed and had its parishioners transferred to the new edifice. Lefevere wanted not only to build a grand cathedral, but he also wanted to "Americanize" the church in Detroit, to wean it from the old French church customs of Ste. Anne parish, founded when Cadillac and the French settled Detroit. He also wanted his cathedral to be an English-speaking parish.

Throughout its history, the parish helped introduce immigrant communities to America. Its initial parishioners were of Irish descent, even wealthy by the standards of the day. From the 1860s onward came new settlers from Germany and Belgium. In 1898, a Kentucky-born Jesuit, Fr. Ferdinand Weinman, was assigned to Detroit, and he helped minister to new immigrants from Sicily and the Middle Eastern countries now known as Lebanon and Syria. As newcomers to this country, they were not warmly welcomed by all at the parish.

In a 1948 history of the parish, Sister M. Therese of the Holy Child described how Ss. Peter and Paul parishioners had a derogatory view of immigrants in the early 1900s:

> There were three definite social divisions of the Jesuit Parish of Sts. Peter & Paul at the turn of the twentieth century. The quality folk, of course, lived on Jefferson Avenue in view of the church. North of Jefferson as far as Champlain Street lived the second strata of society, respectable, hard-working people who formed the backbone of the parish. Down near Hastings and Rivard towards the river were huddled the shacks of the poor. These formed the third and troublesome elements during the century's first decade. Fights were common, as gangs formed to persecute the upper classes. Soon toughness was a virtue to be boasted of. Petty thefts, unruly behavior, and police dodging were feats of heroism.

That referred to the immigrant neighborhoods where Father Weinman ministered. Because of a badly healed broken hip, Weinman limped as he walked. He hobbled along streets and spoke to the residents in the Italian he learned. He gave daily Bible lessons after ringing a small handbell to call children to his side while he sat on house steps to deliver Bible stories. Weinman conducted his ministry in a barn owned by parishioner Francis Palms, Michigan's largest landowner in the 1850s and for whom the Palms Building and the old Palms Theatre were named. After Weinman died in 1906, the Weinman Club of Ss. Peter and Paul Church women opened the Weinman Settlement House on East Larned Street to continue his work. It was the forerunner to the services provided by the League of Catholic Women, now known as Matrix Human Services.

Those immigrant communities later developed the footings to establish new parishes. The Sicilian Italians, led by an Italian Jesuit priest, dedicated Holy Family Catholic Church in 1915 just a few blocks away from Ss. Peter and Paul, and it is still in operation today. Similarly, Middle Eastern immigrants established St. Maron Maronite Catholic Church in 1916 at East Congress and Orleans Streets, where it remained until moving in 1962 to its current location at Kercheval Avenue and St. Jean Street on Detroit's east side.

Ss. Peter and Paul parishioners included educational pioneer Josephine Van Dyke Brownson, who was the first person to organize religious education programs for Catholic children who attended public schools. Her program was known as the Catholic Instruction League, the forerunner to what is often referred to as catechism classes. She developed textbooks for techniques to teach the Catholic faith, and she was honored with the Pro Ecclesia et Pontifice Medal by Pope Pius XI in 1933 and the Laetare Medal in 1939 from Notre Dame.

It is hard to imagine that in the 1970s, Detroit's oldest church was on the brink of closing. The city faced a number of challenges, including a declining population, rising crime, racial unrest, and a struggling economy. By the 1960s, the downtown area had become mainly commercial. With urban renewal and freeway construction, the parish lost its neighborhood and much of its congregation. Around 1970, a decision was made by the Jesuits' Detroit Province to close the parish and allow the University of Detroit to convert the church into a law school library. On February 13, 1972, parishioners glumly gathered for the so-called "Last Mass" at the historic church. "Some of you have come, as it were, to a funeral," Fr. Clement Singer, the Jesuit pastor, told them as he began his sermon. But the gloom was soon replaced by surprised jubilation. Jesuit superiors had decided to keep the parish open, Singer announced. But legal struggles over control of the church property continued for several years. Parishioners sued over whether the church belonged to the University of Detroit or belonged to Ss. Peter and Paul parish. After a long court fight, a judge sided with parishioners, a decision that blessedly occurred on June 29, 1978, the parish's anniversary date.

For years, the church was a place where downtown office workers would stop to pray, enjoy spiritual respite, or attend an Ash Wednesday service on their lunch break. Among those said to have worshiped here were Cora Young, the mother of the city's first African American mayor, Coleman Young, and automotive mogul Henry Ford II after he converted to Catholicism for his marriage. When construction of Detroit's Renaissance Center began in 1973 and the first of five towers opened in 1976, more people found their way to the church.

The gleaming mirrored shine of the Renaissance Center, the tallest building in Michigan, was designed in the 1970s to lift the city's image and project revitalization and renewal. The stocky brick outlines of Ss. Peter and Paul Jesuit Church offers not only an architectural counterpoint but an entirely different perspective on resilience and rejuvenation.

As much as this book celebrates Ss. Peter and Paul's legacy, it is inspiring to document its modern-day impact and foundation for the future. The church has a vibrant congregation. It hails from all over the metropolitan Detroit area. The city's downtown has become a residential hotspot destination for young adults, and the church offers innovative programs to welcome them.

In the tradition of outreach exemplified by Father Weinman, the parish prioritizes service to the poor and disadvantaged. In recent decades, the church opened its hallways and spare spaces to serve as a warming center for those experiencing homelessness. The church's St. Catherine Chapel has been converted to the Pope Francis Center, which provides food, clothing, laundry, and shower services to some 200 people daily. That commitment is visible to the folks who gather outside the Pope Francis Center and is reflected in the statue known as *Homeless Jesus* near the church steps fronting Jefferson Avenue.

Ss. Peter and Paul's history of outreach and service has attracted parishioners from communities across metropolitan Detroit. Carol Goll wandered into the church after a business meeting across the street at the Renaissance Center in the early 1980s looking for a new spiritual home after her previous parish closed. She wanted to be part of a progressive congregation. "I was struck by the beauty inside the plain-looking building. When I went to Mass there the following Sunday with my mother, we were given a very warm greeting right off the bat," said Goll. "The congregation was small at the time. Maybe that's what gave it a family feel." She has been an active member ever since, singing in the choir and chronicling parish history. "Ss. Peter and Paul has been a major part of my life and has loving, welcoming people who reach out to others," says Goll. "They're 'people for others' in the Jesuit tradition."

Ss. Peter and Paul's operations director Lydia Maola joined the parish in 2008. "So much of who I am is this place," Maola said. "This is a place of home for me. I love the history and the architecture. I love that we have a church in a city in the middle of a revival. I love that we are home to many—no matter your walk of life, we can provide something you need."

As it celebrates 175 years since its opening in 1848, the parish community is grateful and growing. Fr. Gary Wright, the Jesuit priest who became Ss. Peter and Paul's pastor in 2015, is inspired by the church's history: "Telling the story of Ss. Peter and Paul's past has made me more in awe than ever of the great people on whose shoulders we stand, and the great legacy we've inherited. But perhaps even more awesome is the potential we have now as a growing presence in downtown Detroit. We are living witnesses that faith in Christ and our Jesuit spirituality still bring forth new life and enable us to be a welcoming presence for all who come, and still empower us to offer ourselves in service to others."

One

A CATHEDRAL
FOR DETROIT

When Bishop Peter Paul Lefevere laid the cornerstone for Detroit's new Catholic cathedral on June 29, 1844, Detroit was a city of about 11,000. Only seven years earlier, in 1837, Michigan had achieved statehood. Detroit was experiencing growing pains. The city's budget was in the red, and it could not afford a police department, according to a 1969 *Detroit Free Press* article. Because of the city's growth, however, Lefevere wanted a grander place for Catholics to worship. There were three other Catholic congregations established in the city at the time: Ste. Anne de Detroit, Most Holy Trinity, and what is now Old St. Mary's in Greektown. But none of those structures captured the grandeur and size of a cathedral, the headquarters or seat of the Catholic faith in the region. Those three other Catholic parishes are still active in Detroit today, but none of them remain in the structures they inhabited when Ss. Peter and Paul's cornerstone went into the ground.

ST. PETERS CATHEDRAL.
DETROIT.

This image represents the first rendering of the design for what was to become Detroit's new Catholic cathedral. It is dated 1845 and bears the name of the Catholic bishop, Peter Paul Lefevere, who ordered the Cathedral's construction. The design included a soaring spire, which was never built, to define its mark on the metropolis's main streets, Jefferson Avenue and St. Antoine Street. The design refers to the building only as St. Peter Cathedral. Much like the city's municipal coffers, the Catholic Church in Detroit was also short on cash. The financial condition of the Detroit bishop's office was on par with the city's dire financial straits. Lefevere only allowed construction to progress when he had the dollars to pay for it. It took four years from ground-breaking to the cathedral's dedication.

Bishop Peter Paul Lefevere had the church consecrated on June 29, 1848, the feast day for the Catholic saints after whom he was named. The feast day recognizes two believers considered pillars of the Roman Catholic Church. St. Peter is considered the father or rock of the Catholic Church, and St. Paul was one of its greatest and earliest evangelists who wrote much of the New Testament. Legend has it that they were both martyred on June 29 during the reign of Emperor Nero and his persecution of followers of Jesus Christ. Lefevere was the leader of Catholics in a diocese that stretched from Michigan to include what is now Iowa and Wisconsin. He died on a cot on March 4, 1869, at St. Mary's Hospital, the city's first hospital, run by Daughters of Charity nuns. His remains were placed in a metallic casket, and he was laid to rest in a vault built under Ss. Peter and Paul's main aisle, about 10 feet from the communion rail of the church he had built and loved so well. His burial site was excavated in 1939 and transferred to Holy Sepulchre Cemetery in the Detroit suburb of Southfield. (Courtesy of the Sisters, Servants of the Immaculate Heart of Mary Archives.)

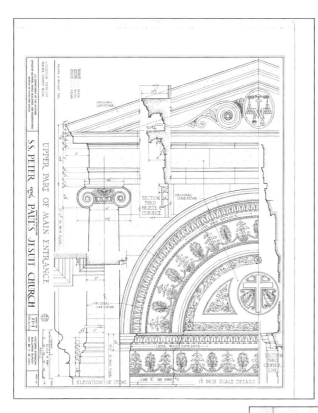

The cathedral was designed in the Romanesque Revival style by architect Francis Latourneau in consultation with Bishop Lefevere's vicar-general, Peter Kindekens, who supervised its construction. This architectural drawing was among those submitted for a 1939 Historic American Buildings Survey. The cathedral was 80 feet across and extended 160 feet from front to back, from Jefferson Avenue to Larned Street.

The stone and masonry work was done by William Burnell, Eustache Chapoton, and George Sanders. This remains the main entrance, and other doors were added decades later. Oak logs from northern Michigan were used for its pillars. In Detroit's *Daily Advertiser*'s directory of 1850–1851, the church was described as being "of the plainest Roman style." In a parish program celebrating the building's 50th anniversary, the author lauded its simple sturdiness, which "has not been surpassed for solidity and plumb."

These registries, pictured above, contain handwritten records of baptisms, weddings, and funeral Masses at Ss. Peter and Paul from its opening in 1848. Below is the handwritten record of the dignitaries who attended the laying of the cathedral's cornerstone in 1844. Bishop Lefevere did some maneuvering to fill the pews when the cathedral opened in 1848. He ordered the closing of nearby Most Holy Trinity Parish, dedicated in 1835 to serve Irish immigrants, and ordered its parishioners to transfer to the new cathedral. For several decades, Ss. Peter and Paul's congregation was almost exclusively of Irish descent. Most Holy Trinity Parish was resurrected in 1849 farther west of downtown to serve the increasing number of Irish immigrants in Detroit's Corktown neighborhood fleeing the Potato Famine. By October 1848, the cathedral had seen the confirmation of 75 girls and boys. (Both photographs by Tom Hagerty Photography.)

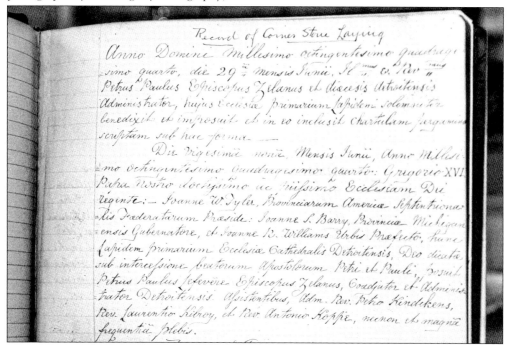

The massive organ with 2,000 pipes, installed in 1848, was constructed by famous organ builder Henry Erben of New York and was heralded as the country's second-largest organ. Erben, who also built the St. Patrick's Cathedral organ in New York City, earned $6,000 for his work in Detroit. The Erben organ was retired from use around 1912, but its pipes remain. The cathedral's first organist was Prof. Peter DeCoster, followed by Prof. Gregory Godfrey Freytag, who played for 45 years until 1916. (Photograph by Tom Hagerty Photography.)

The baptismal font is carved from wood. The first baptism at the cathedral was recorded on January 2, 1849, for Frederick Henry Merritt, whose parents were Isaac Merritt and Eleanore Shehan. Administering the sacrament of baptism was Rev. John Farnan. (Photograph by Mary Schroeder.)

M.*Michael*
212 WOODWARD AVE.
DETROIT

The cathedral's first pastor was the Reverend Edgar Evelyn St. Michael Shawe, an Englishman who fought in the Battle of Waterloo in 1812 against Napoleon's French forces, which ended Napoleon's drive for French domination of Europe. He was ordained a priest in Vincennes, Indiana, and was on the faculty of the University of Notre Dame when Lefevere recruited him to come to Detroit. Shawe died after being thrown from his carriage in an 1851 accident en route to laying the cornerstone for Assumption Grotto Church on the city's east side. Shawe is buried at Mount Elliott Cemetery. An account of his ministry in the 1987 *American Catholic Historical Researches* describes him as an inspiring orator:

> He was a priest who took special pride in having all the ceremonies in the cathedral conducted on a scale worthy of Mother Church; he had the acolytes finely robed, and he drilled them to march with military precision. It was, however, in the pulpit, that this distinguished man appeared to great advantage. His exuberance of ideas proper to the subject; his great command of words, his pathos, his splendid voice, which he knew how to use to advantage, and his vigor of expression, combined to make him a great pulpit orator.

These are among the earliest photographic images of Ss. Peter and Paul, believed to be from around 1860. Above, the church had a prime location astride Jefferson Avenue, and there were many fine residences leading east away from the city's downtown. Below is a stereoscopic image, a type of photography increasingly popular in the 1860s. The image seemed three-dimensional when placed into a viewer or stereoscope, much like the Viewfinder toys familiar to 20th-century generations. (Below, courtesy of the Burton Collection of the Detroit Public Library.)

The cathedral rectory (right) was built at a cost of $11,000 in 1858. The bishop had been living in a residence on Randolph Street a few blocks away from Ss. Peter and Paul. When he left that residence, the Sisters of Charity used the building to house the St. Vincent's Female Orphan Asylum. Below is the wood tribune, also known as the prayer box, which is a hallmark of the east wall of Ss. Peter and Paul. The tribune allowed priests to participate in the Mass and services inside the church without leaving the rectory. The rectory facade remains, but the building is now used by the University of Detroit Mercy Law School. (Below, photograph by Tom Hagerty Photography.)

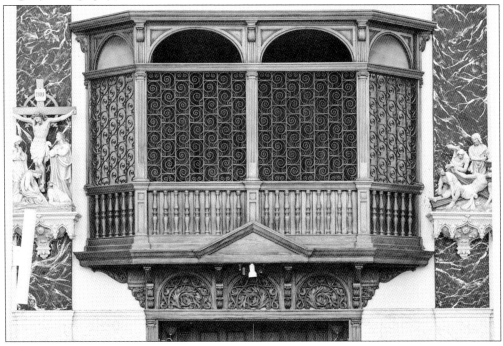

Parishioner Angelo Paldi was among the mural artists for the church. The church's artwork along the ceilings and coves has changed over the decades. Paintings visible to this day are of Ss. Peter and Paul, some of the apostles, and Gospel writers such as St. Mark and St. Luke. Paldi painted his murals on pieces of canvas, which were stretched across the church ceiling. (Photograph by Mary Schroeder.)

Bishop Lefevere was not happy with several elements of the church's construction. He found the 12 massive columns supporting the roof to be out of proportion. He complained that the acoustics were poor and churchgoers could not hear him from the pulpit, placed at the church's center. In 1857, Lefevere had the columns reduced by one third and moved the pulpit closer to the altar at the communion rail. He also had arches installed along the ceiling. This photograph illustrates some of those changes.

20

One of the city's first churches for African Americans is pictured here in the 1860s. Visible just one block away is the back of Ss. Peter and Paul Cathedral. Members of St. Matthew's Episcopal Church, built in 1851 at St. Antoine and Congress Streets, were instrumental in the Underground Railroad, aiding escaped slaves from the South to cross the Detroit River into Canada. The church is described on the photograph's back as a "small wood-paneled building, glass windows with shutters open. Hebrew writing above doorway. Streetlamp and dirt road in foreground. . . . Original St. Matthew's P.E. [Protestant Episcopal] church, built in 1851." In the late 1840s, Black Detroiters purchased a lot at the corner of St. Antoine and Congress Streets to build the small wood church. At one point, the congregation paid $2.22 in taxes for the property. One of the church's leaders, local businessman William Lambert, founded the Colored Vigilant Committee, which coordinated with other African Americans and some white residents to help runaway Southern slaves. The congregation sold the building in 1864 to the Jewish founders of Congregation Shaarey Zedek, numbering 63 members. In 1877, Shaarey Zedek built a new structure on the site, the first time a building was erected in the city for a synagogue. Congregation Shaarey Zedek is now located in Southfield. The historic African American congregation of St. Matthew's is now known as St. Matthew's and St. Joseph's Episcopal Church on Woodward Avenue at Holbrook Avenue. In 2015, the National Park Service included St. Matthew's and St. Joseph's on its National Underground Railroad Network to Freedom. (Courtesy of the Burton Collection of the Detroit Public Library.)

Edward T. Sherlock lived next door to the church and helped run the family-owned grocery. His father, James Sherlock, had been a parishioner at Most Holy Trinity Church in Detroit when Bishop Lefevere ordered parishioners to move to Ss. Peter and Paul, the new cathedral. The Sherlock family home was across the street from their new spiritual home. Edward married Mary Jane Greason at Ss. Peter and Paul on May 1, 1850. He was with the 5th Regiment, Michigan Infantry, known as the Michigan Volunteers, during the Civil War. As lieutenant colonel and commander of the 5th Regiment, he was killed at the Battle of Chancellorsville on May 3, 1863, according to his great-grandson John Brooks Devoe in a letter to the parish. Many parishioners served in the Union army. Parishioner Thornton Brodhead was a commander of the 1st Michigan Cavalry and a onetime postmaster general under Pres. Franklin Pierce. Maj. Angelo Paldi, the parish muralist, and Capt. William Elliott, who was killed in 1863 in action at Fairfield Gap, Virginia, also served in the 1st Michigan Cavalry. Maj. Robert T. Elliott, a commander of the 16th Michigan Infantry, was killed in action at Topomotomy Creek, Virginia, in 1864. (Left, courtesy of the Michigan State Archives; below, courtesy of the Burton Collection of the Detroit Public Library.)

Two

A Jesuit Foundation

Bearing witness from the northwest corner of the church, this statue symbolizes a turning point for Ss. Peter and Paul parish and, indeed, for the city of Detroit. The statue depicts St. Ignatius of Loyola, who was born in the Basque region of Spain in 1491. He was the youngest of 13 children in a Catholic family. As a soldier for Spain at war with France, a leg was shattered by a cannonball during the Battle of Pamplona in 1521. His injury led to introspection and ignited a passionate commitment to his Catholic faith. He studied theology, was ordained a priest, and founded the religious order known as the Society of Jesus, more commonly known as the Jesuits, on September 27, 1540. He is known for his spiritual exercises, which are a set of meditations, prayers, and contemplative practices that are meant to help people grow in their relationship with God. He was 64 when he died in Rome in 1556. Jesuit priests and brothers became known as missionaries and also as educators, the first priestly order to prioritize establishing schools and colleges as a ministry. When Jesuit priests arrived at Ss. Peter and Paul in 1877, they changed the city's landscape. (Photograph by Tom Hagerty Photography.)

Lefevere's successor as bishop of Detroit was Caspar Henry Borgess, a German-born priest. Borgess served in Detroit from 1870 to 1887. He entered the priesthood after immigrating to America and studied under the Jesuits in Cincinnati. As a young priest, he ministered to those suffering from cholera during an epidemic in Columbus, Ohio. When he wanted to open a Catholic college in Detroit, he turned to the Jesuits. Borgess invited them to return to Detroit—a Jesuit priest was among the Europeans who arrived with Antoine Cadillac to establish a settlement in 1701. Borgess offered to give the Jesuits the cathedral parish of Ss. Peter and Paul in 1877. The Jesuits accepted, and Borgess deeded over the title and transferred the cathedral's ministry several blocks away to St. Aloysius, a parish founded a few years earlier in 1873. The Jesuit community continues to own the church property. That is not the case for other Catholic parishes in the area, with each church property owned by the Archdiocese of Detroit. (Courtesy of the Sisters, Servants of the Immaculate Heart of Mary Archives.)

This c. 1880 image captures the church much as the Jesuits inherited it. Detroit's population was about 115,000. Nearly half of the city's population was made up of immigrants from an estimated 40 nations, according to the Detroit Historical Society. About this same time, entrepreneurs were establishing landmark businesses. Frederick Sanders opened an ice cream and candy shop on Woodward Avenue. The first J.L. Hudson store opened on the ground floor of the long-gone Detroit Opera House. And Alexander Graham Bell's invention of the telephone brought the first telephone exchange to the city for 124 customers. The land that holds Ss. Peter and Paul Jesuit Church rests on ancestral land of the Anishinaabeg Three Fires Confederacy: the Ojibwa, Odawa, and Potawatomi Nations. In the early 1700s, French colonial settlers appropriated the land, and in the 1840s, the Diocese of Detroit received this property as a gift from the estate of Antoine Beaubien, a settler descendant whose family's wealth was built in part by the labor of indigenous people they held in slavery. The current Ss. Peter and Paul parish community believes it is important to acknowledge this to illustrate current Catholic and Jesuit commitments to justice and reconciliation. It represents a gesture of respect and a small step toward correcting the stories and practices that erase indigenous people's history and culture, says parish pastor Fr. Gary Wright. "It calls us to understand the history that led to our parish's presence on this land," says Wright, "and demands that we strengthen our parish commitment to equity and advancement for all people in our community today."

REV. J. B. MIEGE, S. J.,
PRESIDENT DETROIT COLLEGE,
1877 – 1880.

The first Jesuit steward of Ss. Peter and Paul Church was the Right Reverend John Miege, who had been the Catholic bishop of Leavenworth, Kansas, and was lauded as "one of the most heroic missionaries on the plains and 'Rockies' of the Wild West," as described in an 1898 parish retrospective.

FR. JAMES WALSHE, S. J.

Miege was accompanied by Fr. James J. Walshe. Miege and Walshe arrived in May 1877 and held their first service on June 3 at Ss. Peter and Paul. For parishioners, they launched such organizations as the League of the Sacred Heart, the Society for a Happy Death, the Perpetual Adoration Society, and clubs for "Men, Married Ladies and Young Ladies," according to an 1898 parish retrospective. (Courtesy of the Jesuit Archives & Research Center.)

On June 16, 1877, the Jesuits purchased a residence at 630 East Jefferson Avenue known as the Trowbridge House (above) for $21,500, comparable to more than $500,000 today. On September 3, it opened as Detroit College. It functioned initially as a high school. Some 60 students enrolled, and its first entrant was William J. St. Aubin. This house also launched what is today the University of Detroit Mercy and the University of Detroit Jesuit High School. In the coming years, the Jesuits acquired other properties along Jefferson Avenue near Ss. Peter and Paul to accommodate growing enrollment. By 1890, the Jesuits built the facility below next to the church for the main building of Detroit College, still in use today as the University of Detroit Mercy Law School. (Both, courtesy of the University of Detroit Mercy Archives.)

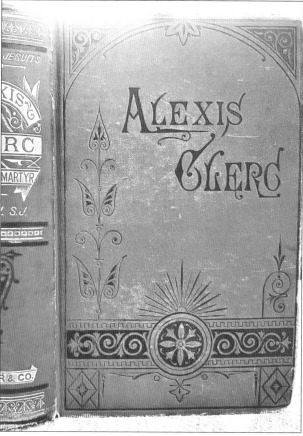

Charles P. Friederichs Jr., born in 1866 in Detroit to German and Swiss immigrants, attended Detroit College for high school. For his mastery of history and geography, he was awarded this book about Jesuit priest Fr. Alexis LeClerc (left). When Detroit College opened, the school day began at 8:30 with Mass, then studies in Latin, Greek, penmanship, religious instruction, math, English, history, and geography. Free days were Thursday and Sunday. Tuition at Detroit College was $40. Friederichs's family operated a stained glass studio in the city, founded as Friederichs and Staffin in 1861 and later known as Detroit Stained Glass Works. The firm designed windows for such landmark churches as Old St. Mary in Greektown and Detroit St. Joseph. Friederichs is pictured above outside the stained glass studio, located on Gratiot Avenue. He worked in the family business until his death in 1937. (Both, courtesy of Paul G. Diehl.)

The altar boys above were adorned in lace for the Christmas Mass of 1886 at Ss. Peter and Paul, when Bishop Caspar Borgess, the main celebrant, remarked, "I have not been so pleased with anything since the Jesuits came to Detroit to open the school." Assisting at that Christmas Mass was another Jesuit, the Reverend Thomas Sherman, son of the Civil War general William T. Sherman. Below is another photograph of altar boys and a Jesuit priest from that time period.

A side altar with statues depicting St. Ignatius, Jesus, and St. Francis Xavier was added to the church in 1882. St. Francis Xavier was one of the first members of the Jesuit order and was a missionary in Asia, including India and Japan. The east side altar includes statues of Mary, the Mother of Jesus, and St. Aloysius Gonzaga and St. Stanislaus Kostka, both Jesuits. (Photograph by Tom Hagerty Photography.)

Ss. Peter and Paul parishioners in 1897 were prosperous and active. They were mostly of Irish and German descent, and among them were some of Detroit's most successful businessmen and ladies of society. The neighborhood also was becoming home to Italian and Middle Eastern immigrants. This booklet described the activities available to parishioners. The booklet cover showcases the letters A.M.D.G.—*Ad Majorem Dei Glorium* in Latin or "For the Greater Glory of God." It is the Jesuit motto and refers to a philosophy of doing more for others in the spirit of Jesus.

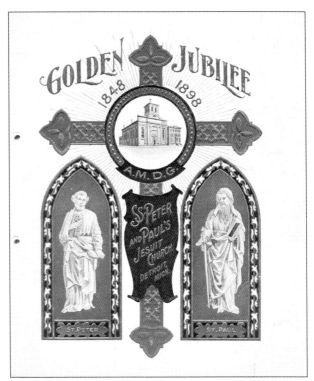

At right is the booklet from the parish's Golden Jubilee on May 28, 1899. The Golden Jubilee was supposed to mark the 50-year anniversary from the church's opening in 1848, but the celebration actually coincided with the church's 51st anniversary. The celebration was delayed a year because of the Spanish-American War. At the time of the jubilee, there was a proposal to rebuild the church's front exterior in stone and crown it with a spire for $25,000, but nothing came of it. Below is a glimpse of the church's interior in 1899.

Ss. Peter and Paul served as the spiritual home for the students at the adjacent Detroit College, the forerunner to today's University of Detroit Mercy and University of Detroit Jesuit High School. This is the Detroit College baseball team of 1889, coached by a young Jesuit. (Courtesy of the University of Detroit Mercy Archives.)

In 1908, a new altar depicting Jesus's crucifixion was installed. A parish family, the Fleitzes, donated $25,000 to memorialize onetime parishioner Elizabeth M. Fleitz, the wife of John P. Fleitz, a prominent leader in the lumber and grain industries. A relic of St. Francis Borgia, a Jesuit priest and saint, was added to other relics transferred from the old altar. The altar was designed by a local architect, Gustave Mueller. Carrara marble, quarried in Italy, was shipped to New York to be finished by noted church sculptor Joseph Sibbel, who died shortly after completing the work considered his final masterpiece. It was installed in Detroit by the American Marble Company of Vermont. The altar is 39 feet high, 26 feet wide, and weighs 17 tons. It took six months to reconstruct it here. (Courtesy of the Walter P. Reuther Library, Wayne State University.)

"Uncle George" writes that he "sang here for a while" in a 1908 postcard featuring Ss. Peter and Paul with a horse buggy parked out front. On the postcard below, depicting the church and the adjacent Detroit College classrooms, the writer describes that the church at the corner of St. Antoine Street and Jefferson Avenue is "where I tell my troubles." (Both, courtesy of Dan Austin, HistoricDetroit.org)

A 3851 a. Jesuit Church, Detroit, Mich.

Sang here for awhile
Something alike 18" s Girard Ave
8/16/08 Uncle George.

Detroit Apr 14·07.

Mayme. Rogers is better, but is not going to make Chicago this week. Had to send another man on a/c of his illness. Hope you are well.

Where I tell my troubles.

Jesuit church St Antoine and Jefferson ave's cor'dr Detroit College

In 1918, the Jesuits added St. Catherine Chapel to the back of the church, used primarily as the worship space for Detroit College students. It was built with donations from the Dinan family. The lettering A.M.D.G. adorning the chapel's entrance expresses bedrock Jesuit philosophy. St. Ignatius Loyola adopted the use of the monogram IHS, derived from the Greek spelling of Jesus, as the Jesuits' seal. The chapel also served as a worship site for a growing number of Lebanese and Syrian immigrants at the turn of the 20th century and was used for mixed-religion marriages before the reforms of Vatican II allowed such ceremonies in the main sanctuary. The chapel has been remodeled to provide laundry, showering, and dining facilities for the Pope Francis Center, which aids homeless and disadvantaged people. (Below, photograph by Mary Schroeder.)

Three

THE PARISH SCHOOL

Since it opened its doors, Ss. Peter and Paul Church has prided itself on its instruction of Catholic teaching to those in the pews. It also sought to teach elementary basics to youngsters. A parish school for boys was established in 1856. The Christian Brothers were the instructors until 1859; they were then replaced by lay teachers until 1864. Catholic sisters also were recruited to provide instruction in the years that followed. In 1887, Ss. Peter and Paul Elementary School, which first served just boys, was erected at the cost of $38,000 on Larned Street behind the school. (Courtesy of Jesuit Archives & Research Center.)

Among the first Catholic nuns to teach here were the Sisters, Servants of the Immaculate Heart of Mary congregation, commonly known as the IHMs and founded in Monroe, Michigan, in 1845. Sister Clotilda Hoskyns became an IHM in 1863 at the age of 21 and taught at Ss. Peter and Paul from 1864 to 1868. Some 30 children were present on the first day of school in January 1865. Tuition was 10¢ a week, reduced to 5¢ "for smaller pupils," according to the IHM records. Hoskyns became the congregation's mother superior when she was just 28. She died in 1914. (Courtesy of the Sisters, Servants of the Immaculate Heart of Mary Archive.)

Sister Catherine Biry, an IHM sister, was at the school from 1868 to 1870 after teaching one year at St. Augustine School, established to teach Black children at nearby St. Mary's Parish, now known as Old St. Mary's in Greektown. Biry was born in Bern, Switzerland, in 1844 and entered the IHMs in Monroe at the age of 15. Biry was the last woman accepted into the IHMs by the congregation's cofounder, Sister Theresa Maxis Duchemin. Duchemin was forced to leave Michigan because she had angered Bishop Lefevere, in part because he found out she was biracial and had descended from enslaved Black Haitians. The IHMs taught at Ss. Peter and Paul until the early 1880s. (Courtesy of the Sisters, Servants of the Immaculate Heart of Mary Archive.)

Nuns who belonged to the order of the Society of the Sacred Heart of Jesus, also known by the initials RSCJ based on the order's French name, were among the pioneering congregations to establish schools in Detroit. Sacred Heart nuns taught girls associated with Ss. Peter and Paul parish as early as the late 1850s–1860s. In 1862, the congregation erected a building on Jefferson Avenue near the cathedral, pictured above. The school, run by the Sacred Heart nuns, some of whom are pictured below, served partly as an elite girls' academy where French was the preferred language, an orphanage, and an English language school for Ss. Peter and Paul parish girls, according to a history provided by the congregation. (Both, courtesy of the Society of the Sacred Heart United States–Canada Province Archives.)

CHAS. ZEIGLER ARCHIE FREY   BRITT WHITMAN   ANTHONY KAISER GERALD FITZ GIBBONS LEO HEADHY
ROBT. KELLY   JOS. MARR   RICHARD MAHER   GEORGE RENO   JOHN RABAUT   EUGENE LOOK JAS GUINAN
FRANCIS LOOK   NEIL OTTO   THOS. STACKPOLE EUGENE VAN ANTWERP FRED SCHIAPPACASSE ARTHUR KRATZ ELMER SCHNEIDER
LEO RABAUT   BERNARD STORM DUFFIELD STORM ARTHUR STORM VINCENT BRENNAN JAS. COLFORD WM. SWEENEY

Parish schoolboys pose for a photograph near the turn of the 20th century. Their names, listed at the bottom of the photograph, attest to how Ss. Peter and Paul parishioners were predominantly of Irish, German, and Belgian heritage in the late 1800s. This photograph captures some prominent Detroiters when they were schoolboys. Eugene Van Antwerp (second row, center) was elected to the Detroit Common Council in 1931, served as the city's mayor in 1948–1949, and returned to the council from 1951 until his death in August 1962. George Reno (third row, center) became a Jesuit priest. He was a college student at Detroit College when it underwent a name change in 1911 and became known as the University of Detroit. Reno was in the 1914 graduating class and became a longtime administrator at the University of Detroit, from 1926 to 1950. Reno Hall dormitory on the campus is named after him. Vincent Brennan (first row, third from right) was a noted city lawyer credited with drafting automobile traffic ordinances that became national models. He was a Wayne County Circuit Court judge from 1924 to 1954. When these students were at Ss. Peter and Paul Elementary School, the parish community was changing, as immigrants from Italy and the Middle East were moving into the area.

Sisters of Charity from Cincinnati commenced teaching at Ss. Peter and Paul Elementary School on January 3, 1888, as instructors for 125 boys. Sister Coains McCadden (right) was among the Sisters of Charity who taught in Detroit. She joined the congregation under the leadership of St. Elizabeth Ann Seton, who when known as Mother Seton was considered the founder of the parochial school system in the United States. Sister Coains was considered one of Seton's pioneer Catholic school teachers. The sisters' convent (below) was adjacent to the school. (Right, courtesy of the Sisters of Charity of Cincinnati Archives.)

Words from Matthew 19:14 were inscribed over the school door (above). "Suffer the little children. Come unto me" is derived from Matthew's recording of Jesus preaching that the Kingdom of Heaven belongs to people who display the kindness and openness of children. Above, two Sisters of Charity are seen in front of the school. Below, an unnamed sister poses with altar boys from the school. (Both, courtesy of the Sisters of Charity of Cincinnati Archives.)

Sister Alphonse Gallagher was the longest-serving teacher at Ss. Peter and Paul Elementary School. She taught for 52 years, from 1896 to 1897 and from 1913 to 1964. At the age of 87, as the school neared closing, she returned to Cincinnati. In 1961, the church arranged a solemn High Mass and open house for her in recognition of 50 years of teaching at the school. (Courtesy of the Sisters of Charity of Cincinnati Archives.)

Sister Alphonse also was honored when Dearborn-based radio station WKMH announced her name at 11:05 a.m. on its June 26, 1961, broadcast. The station also sent her a flower arrangement with best wishes for "her valuable services, upon the recommendation of many friends." An article in the publication *Catholic Telegraph* noted that Sister Alphonse "had taught a child at SS. Peter and Paul, whose father and grandfather had been in her classes before him." (Courtesy of the Sisters of Charity of Cincinnati Archives.)

These are the eighth graders who matriculated at Ss. Peter and Paul Grade School in 1923. From left to right are (top row) Joseph Moreno, Sophy Serie, Harry Pine, George Michales, Nick Lentine, Gustava Ansaneeuw, and Angelo Moreno; (middle row) Anna Peters, Josephine Mozzola, Joseph Fodell, Joseph Ellias, Michael "Ti" Joseph, Joseph Rizk, Anthony Catalano, and John Tedesco; (bottom row) Margaret Wayne, Anthony Gerada, David Edwards, Louis Basharrah, Fritz Foravazo, Samuel Masola, and Anthony Catalano. Michael Joseph survived being aboard the *Titanic* during its ill-fated crossing of the Atlantic in 1912. The sisters nicknamed him "Ti" in reference to the

doomed ship. He recounted the sense that, separated from his mother on board, he was saved by a guardian angel. Born in Lebanon, he was traveling with his mother, Catherine, and his sister, Mary, to join their father in the United States. Their tickets were among the least expensive, putting them on the ship's lower deck. His mother told him to "hang on my skirt tails" when the ship started to sink, but he became separated. "It was then that the guardian angel grabbed my hand and I was placed in a lifeboat," he recounted. He was reunited with his mother and sister on Ellis Island. When he died in May 1991, his funeral Mass was at Ss. Peter and Paul.

The nuns who arrived to teach in Detroit were among the first sisters of their Cincinnati-based congregation to teach outside of Ohio. This is Sister Anne Loretto Connell, who was a principal at the school. When the Sisters of Charity assumed direction of the parish school in 1888, Sister Maria Louise Hebert was the first principal. (Courtesy of the Sisters of Charity of Cincinnati.)

Sister Beatrice Anne Garlock (far left) was a principal at the school and is pictured here with her parents and her sister, also a Sister of Charity, Sister Maria Garlock. (Courtesy of the Sisters of Charity of Cincinnati Archives.)

Sister Francis Solano McCarthy was the last principal of the school when it closed in 1964. The school had struggled with expenses and dwindling enrollment over the years, and many students came from families with low incomes. The sisters sought clothing and donations from more prosperous suburban parishes.

This May 1961 photograph shows several sisters posing with a student who is making her First Communion. From left to right are Sisters of Charity Beatrice Anne Garlock, Mary Conchessa Mulroy, Alphonse Gallagher, an unidentified student, and Sister Eugene Mary Donohue.

45

This view of downtown Detroit is from Ss. Peter and Paul Grade School on Larned Street, a few blocks east of downtown office buildings, in the 1950s. The school, which was run by the Sisters of Charity of Cincinnati for 94 years, closed in 1964 and was later demolished. As the school building was being prepared for demolition, statues of saints were removed from the classrooms.

Four

THE JESUIT IMPRINT GROWS

From 1910 to 1930, Detroit experienced explosive growth because of the new auto industry's transformation of travel. The city's population doubled from 1910 to one million in 1920 and then grew by another 600,000 by 1930. Many of the city's new citizens were immigrants from European countries who were Catholics. Detroit Catholic bishop Michael Gallagher (above) oversaw the construction of multiple new parishes and Catholic schools in the area. At the Jesuit-run University of Detroit next door to Ss. Peter and Paul Jesuit Church, classrooms were bursting with students. The 1920s heralded a period when the Jesuits expanded their outreach and footprint in the Detroit area. Detroit annexed several outlying areas past the existing city limits. In 1921, the Reverend John P. McNichols, president of he University of Detroit, purchased farmland about six miles north of Ss. Peter and Paul to relocate the institution. In this photograph, Bishop Gallagher breaks ground on Thanksgiving Day 1925 for a new campus for the University of Detroit. (Courtesy of the University of Detroit Mercy Archives.)

Follow the streetcars down through the center of the above photograph and the eye will arrive at the familiar outlines of Ss. Peter and Paul Jesuit Church, its front exterior topped off by a cross. This was Jefferson Avenue in the mid-1920s, when the Jesuits began to expand their ministry and educational stewardship. Below is another view of the Jefferson Avenue neighborhood around Ss. Peter and Paul Jesuit Church and the adjoining University of Detroit, which educated teenage boys and college students. (Above, courtesy of the Detroit Historical Society; below, courtesy of the University of Detroit Mercy Archives.)

Fr. John McNichols, pictured below as a young priest, was president of the University of Detroit from 1921 until his death in 1932. He is believed to be pictured in the above photograph to the right of Detroit bishop Michael Gallagher at the 1925 groundbreaking for the new college campus along Livernois Avenue at its intersection with Six Mile Road. His death was front-page news, and he was lauded for his contributions to Michigan's first, oldest, and biggest Catholic university. His funeral Mass was attended by 150 priests at Ss. Peter and Paul Jesuit Church. After he died, the city renamed Six Mile Road after him. (Above, courtesy of the University of Detroit Mercy Archives; below, courtesy of the Jesuit Archive & Research Center.)

The *Detroit News* recorded the campus groundbreaking on its front page. With the turn of a silver spade, "the physical beginning was made to the new $8,000,000 plant" sure "to make educational history for the city and state." The groundbreaking portended "a group of massive and dignified buildings housing thousands of students and upholding the standards of education, which have been carried for nearly 50 years by the university under less ample facilities." This photograph includes the campus's iconic clock tower. (Courtesy of the University of Detroit Mercy Archives.)

This image from the 1960s includes an overview of the long-gone football stadium at the University of Detroit, which is now known as the University of Detroit Mercy after the it merged with nearby Mercy College in 1990. (Courtesy of the University of Detroit Mercy Archives.)

Father McNichols also established the University of Detroit's graduate school and its school of dentistry. Here is one of the early buildings that housed the dental school and the university's business and commerce programs. The dental school is one of only two in Michigan and has a long history of outreach to disadvantaged populations. In the 1964 photograph below, children receive check-ups at the dental school. (Above, courtesy of the University of Detroit Mercy Archives; below, courtesy of the *Detroit Free Press*.)

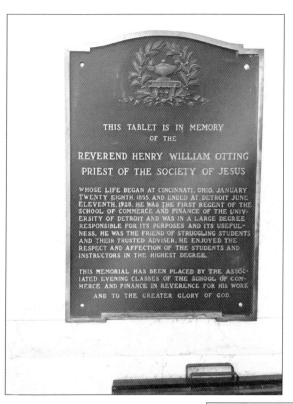

THIS TABLET IS IN MEMORY
OF THE

REVEREND HENRY WILLIAM OTTING
PRIEST OF THE SOCIETY OF JESUS

WHOSE LIFE BEGAN AT CINCINNATI, OHIO, JANUARY
TWENTY EIGHTH, 1855, AND ENDED AT DETROIT JUNE
ELEVENTH, 1928. HE WAS THE FIRST REGENT OF THE
SCHOOL OF COMMERCE AND FINANCE OF THE UNIV-
ERSITY OF DETROIT AND WAS IN A LARGE DEGREE
RESPONSIBLE FOR ITS PURPOSES AND ITS USEFUL-
NESS. HE WAS THE FRIEND OF STRUGGLING STUDENTS
AND THEIR TRUSTED ADVISER. HE ENJOYED THE
RESPECT AND AFFECTION OF THE STUDENTS AND
INSTRUCTORS IN THE HIGHEST DEGREE.

THIS MEMORIAL HAS BEEN PLACED BY THE ASSOC-
IATED EVENING CLASSES OF THE SCHOOL OF COM-
MERCE AND FINANCE IN REVERENCE FOR HIS WORK
AND TO THE GREATER GLORY OF GOD.

Tens of thousands of graduates earned degrees in business administration, accounting, finance, and management from the business school first led by the Jesuit Rev. William Henry Otting. This plaque honoring Otting, who died in 1928, hangs in the vestibule of Ss. Peter and Paul. Otting's students commissioned the plaque in appreciation of what he taught them after they walked through the door pictured below, just yards away from the church entrance. (Left, photograph by Visionalist Entertainment.)

Here is the campus nearly a century after McNichols expanded the Jesuits' footprint in Detroit. In the 2021–2022 school year, it enrolled nearly 3,000 undergraduates and 2,300 students pursuing graduate degrees in business, dentistry, law, nursing, health professions, engineering, science, architecture, and the liberal arts. In 1990, the University of Detroit merged with nearby Mercy College, founded by the Sisters of Mercy. Below are three past presidents. At left is Antoine Garibaldi, president from 2012 to 2022 and the first African American to lead the university. At center is the late Sister Maureen Fay, an Adrian Dominican sister who was the first woman and non-Jesuit president. At right is the late Rev. Gerard L. Stockhausen, a Jesuit who served from 2004 to 2010. On July 1, 2022, Donald B. Taylor, PhD, became the 26th president of University of Detroit Mercy. (Both, courtesy of the University of Detroit Mercy Archives.)

In 1926, a group of Catholic laymen worked to establish a place for spiritual renewal rather than travel to Cleveland for silent, contemplative weekend retreats led by the Jesuits. They raised enough funds to buy a country estate. This is the entrance to Manresa Jesuit Retreat Center, 20 miles from downtown Detroit. Its name derives from the Spanish town where a young St. Ignatius Loyola lived for a time as a hermit in a riverside cavern. (Courtesy of the *Detroit Free Press*.)

Fire destroyed the original building used to house retreat participants. The new retreat house, designed in the Cotswold style by architect Alois Herman, was completed in 1936. The Jesuits lead retreats to this day at Manresa. (Courtesy of the *Detroit Free Press*.)

Many men, and women when they were eventually allowed to take part in retreats in the 1940s, were drawn to the bucolic setting. Among its features highlighted in these 1941 photographs were an old gristmill (right) and a grotto (below) dedicated to Mary, the mother of Jesus. Manresa Jesuit Retreat House remains restful and lush with greenery even in the midst of the busy Oakland County intersection of Quarton Road and Woodward Avenue. (Both, courtesy of the *Detroit Free Press*.)

In 1922, the Reverend John McNichols established a new Catholic parish community near the land he purchased to relocate the Jesuits' college from downtown Detroit. On March 19, 1922, McNichols said Mass for about 25 people in a farmhouse (above) that served as the parish church for several years. He named the parish Gesu, the Italian word for Jesus. (Courtesy of the Gesu Parish Archives.)

In 1925, the Gesu Elementary School was opened, and masses were held in its basement until a new Gesu Church was dedicated in 1937. Gesu School remains open to this day, one of only four Catholic elementary schools in Detroit compared to 108 such grade schools in the mid-1960s. (Courtesy of the Sisters, Servants of the Immaculate Heart of Mary Archive.)

Gesu Church was designed by architect George F. Diehl in the Spanish modern style. Its design sought to complement a similar style with the buildings across the street at the University of Detroit. (Courtesy of the Gesu Parish Archives.)

Gesu School students assembled in the school gym in April 2022. The school will celebrate its centennial year of operation in 2025. Gesu School educates pupils from throughout Detroit and suburbs such as Ferndale, Redford, Bloomfield Hills, Southfield, and Sterling Heights. (Photograph by Diane Weiss.)

In 1931, the Jesuits opened a school specifically for teenaged boys on Seven Mile Road, between Wyoming and Livernois Avenues, moving them from classrooms in the building adjacent to Ss. Peter and Paul Church. Its name became the University of Detroit High School, and the school's mascot became the Cubs in reference to the Bears, the mascot then in use at the nearby University of Detroit college. (Courtesy of the University of Detroit Jesuit High School and Academy.)

In 1966, the superior general of the worldwide Jesuit order of priests and brothers, the Reverend Pedro Arrupe (right), visited the University of Detroit High School. Arrupe's tenure from 1965 to 1983 coincided with the modern Catholic Church reforms unleashed by the Second Vatican Council. The Jesuits have commenced an effort that could lead to the eventual canonization of Arrupe as a Catholic saint. (Courtesy of the Jesuit Archive & Research Center.)

The Reverend Malcolm Carron was president of the University of Detroit High School in the mid-1980s. As Detroit's population declined among economic and racial struggles, the Jesuits considered moving the high school outside the city but decided against it. The school added an academy for seventh and eighth graders in the 1970s and is now known as University of Detroit Jesuit High School and Academy. It remains one of only three Catholic high schools in the city, compared to 55 in the mid-1960s. (Photograph by John Collier; courtesy of the *Detroit Free Press*.)

It is an annual tradition for seniors at the University of Detroit Jesuit High School to gather at its stately staircase for an annual portrait. Since its founding by Jesuits at Ss. Peter and Paul parish, the school is the oldest continuously operating high school in Detroit. Its motto is "Men for Others," and the school draws students from more than 70 communities across metro Detroit. (Courtesy of the University of Detroit Jesuit High School and Academy.)

The Jesuits assigned to Ss. Peter and Paul Church and the adjoining Detroit College gathered for this c. 1907 photograph. At far right on the second row, standing slightly apart from the others, is the Reverend Giovanni Boschi, a Sicilian-born Jesuit. He was recruited by the Detroit Jesuits to establish a separate church nearby for the growing numbers of immigrants from Sicilian towns such as Cinisi and Terrasini. (Courtesy of the Jesuit Archive & Research Center.)

Around the corner from Ss. Peter and Paul, a church named Holy Family was built for the Sicilians and dedicated here by Detroit bishop John Foley in 1910. (Courtesy of Bonnie Leone and Holy Family Parish.)

The Reverend Giuseppe Licciardi (above) was pastor of Holy Family parish when this interior photograph was shot in 2013. The church sits on the edge of the I-375 expressway in downtown Detroit (below), and it was photographed in earlier decades silhouetted by fireworks exploding around Detroit's Renaissance Center. There are preliminary plans to remove the expressway to create more walkable surface streets. Its construction destroyed a historic African American neighborhood in the 1960s known as Black Bottom due its rich dark soil. (Above, courtesy of the *Detroit Free Press*; below, courtesy of Bonnie Leone and Holy Family Parish.)

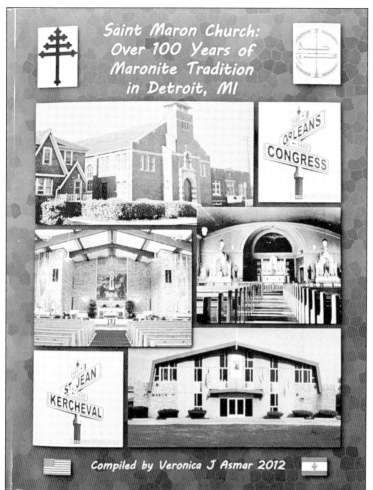

Saint Maron Church:
Over 100 Years of
Maronite Tradition
in Detroit, MI

Compiled by Veronica J Asmar 2012

Ss. Peter and Paul Church also was the spiritual home of Maronite Rite Catholics who immigrated to Detroit in the early 1900s from Lebanon and Syria. In 1915, construction began on a separate church, named after the fourth-century Catholic priest and hermit St. Maron. At left, a book compiled in 2012 depicts the congregation's first and current church. The first church was demolished in the 1960s to make way for urban renewal projects. In 1965, the current St. Maron Church was dedicated at the corner of Kercheval and St. Jean Streets on Detroit's east side. (Below, photograph by Tom Hagerty Photography.)

Isabel Ganem and Paul Saigh were married in 1954 at the original St. Maron Church by the Reverend Michael Abdoo (above). Isabel's father, Fadel Ganem, opened what is considered the first Middle Eastern restaurant in Detroit, The Sheik, where comedian and actor Danny Thomas was a frequent patron and sketched out the idea for St. Jude Children's Hospital. At right, Isabel is pictured at center inside today's St. Maron Church with its pastor, the Reverend Roby Zibara (left), and her nephew, Paul Fadel Ganem (right), who was among the last to be baptized in the old church. (Above, courtesy of Isabel Saigh; right, photograph by Patricia Montemurri.)

In 2008, Detroit Jesuits celebrated a 50-year anniversary to mark the establishment and administration of the Detroit Province. The Society of Jesus is divided into geographic areas called provinces. Across the world, there are more than 60 provinces, but their boundaries and names adapt to reflect the changing number of Jesuits and the institutions they manage. There was a Detroit Province from 1958 to 2014, when it was merged with the Chicago Province to become known as the Chicago-Detroit Province. In 2017, the US Jesuits were divided into four provinces. Jesuits in Michigan are now part of the Midwest Province of Jesuits. The superior general of the Jesuits, Fr. Peter Hans Kolvenbach, visited Detroit in 2008. He is photographed here speaking at Gesu Church, administered by the Jesuits since 1922. At far right is Fr. Gary Wright, then rector of the university Jesuit community and current pastor of Ss. Peter and Paul Church. Next to Wright is the late Fr. Gerard Stockhausen, who was president of the University of Detroit Mercy at the time. (Courtesy of Michael Sarnacki.)

Five

FAITH IN SERVICE

Ss. Peter and Paul Church's pastors and parishioners created a legacy of charity and service throughout its history. One example was the outreach of the Reverend Ferdinand Weinman, who as the church's associate pastor in the 1890s began a special ministry to recent immigrants from Italy and the Middle East. He learned Italian, and Weinman caught the attention of newcomers by walking the streets ringing a handbell to tell Gospel stories. He opened a center for immigrants in a barn owned by a well-to-do parishioner, Francis Palms, who owned the Palms Theatre. Inspired by Weinman's service, a group of Catholic women founded the Weinman Club in 1906 to assist immigrants and moved the programs into this building at 425 East Larned Street. It was called the Weinman Settlement House and provided educational programs and services to Italian, Syrian, and Lebanese immigrants and later the African American community until 1946. In 1911, it came to be operated by the Catholic Settlement Association, which in 1915 became the League of Catholic Women (now known as Matrix Human Services), an organization founded by another parishioner, Annie Casgrain.

Ss. Peter and Paul Church's 1948 centennial celebration booklet vividly described Father Weinman's ministry to immigrants:

> Day after day, Father Weinman painfully limped his way (he had a broken hip, which never knitted correctly) up and down Congress, Larned, Franklin, and even Woodbridge streets. His technique of approach was the ringing of a small hand-bell. . . . At the sound of the bell, children flocked after him, clamoring for their daily lesson in Christian doctrine. Seated on any doorstep, without the aid of desk or book, he captivated their young minds and hearts with the beauty of the Gospel's 'good news.' Not infrequently, little hands would be caught in his bulging pockets, for the little minds knew that in them would be found rich rewards—medals of various shapes and colors.

Father Weinman, the writer noted, "was a familiar figure to all, but he was more than this to the recent immigrant Italians; he was their temporal as well as spiritual director." When Weinman died in August 1907, Detroit bishop John Foley preached at the funeral Mass at Ss. Peter and Paul, and 50 priests of the diocese were present. (Courtesy of the Jesuit Archive & Research Center.)

The Weinman Settlement House provided instruction and activities for youngsters, and music from the piano accompanied playtime activities. Father Weinman had set examples of how to provide outlets to redirect sometimes mischievous youthful energy. "The troublesome ones were fighting but now with gloves and under supervision. Such was the spirit which Father Weinman built into his work," according to an account in the 1948 parish centennial book, entitled *The Glory of Saints Peter and Paul.*

Members of the League of Catholic Women volunteered at operating the Weinman Settlement House, which remained on Larned Street until 1946. Youngsters from the immigrant neighborhoods near Ss. Peter and Paul gather around tables in the undated photograph at left. Volunteers help young women learn English and job skills below.

Children in a kindergarten class at the Weinman Settlement House in 1924 are treated to beverages.

In the mid-1940s, the League of Catholic Women, who operated the Weinman Settlement House, also sought to purchase another facility to provide safe housing for single working women. The Weinman Settlement House closed in 1946 and was eventually demolished. The Weinman Settlement services continued operation at a location on Avery Street in St. Dominic Catholic parish.

Ss. Peter and Paul parishioner Anastasia "Annie" (Hammond) Casgrain is considered the founder of the League of Catholic Women in Detroit, a charitable organization now known as Matrix Human Services. She was a leader in the Catholic Settlement Association, which grew out of the women who banded together as the Weinman Club to help immigrants. In 1912, the Catholic Settlement Association raised money to open a boardinghouse for young immigrant women to obtain low-cost room and board as well as education and job skills. Casgrain offered space in her home on West Lafayette Boulevard free of charge to the women. In 1915, the Catholic Settlement Association was renamed the League of Catholic Women. A building in Detroit's Midtown neighborhood served as the league's headquarters for decades and was named Casgrain Hall. The building was listed in the National Register of Historic Places in 1997 and is a now a senior citizen residence. Casgrain is pictured in front of her portrait.

Educational pioneer Josephine (Van Dyke) Brownson, another parishioner, was the first person to organize religious education programs for children in public schools. She was a Detroit public school math teacher who resigned to design instructional materials to teach Catholic public school children about the foundations of the faith. It was the beginning of programs many knew as catechism or the Confraternity of Christian Doctrine (CCD). She developed texts that were hailed for their quality and rigor. By 1939, the Detroit program she organized included 400 teachers and 13,000 students. She was honored with the Pro Ecclesia et Pontifice Medal by Pope Pius XI. It is the highest honor that can be awarded to a layperson by the pope for distinguished service to the church. She also was awarded the Notre Dame University Laetare Medal, the most prestigious award an American Catholic can receive. The award (pronounced Lay-TAH-ray) is derived from the Latin word for "rejoice." Recipients speak at Notre Dame's commencement ceremonies. Past recipients have included Catholic Worker founder Dorothy Day and Pres. John F. Kennedy.

The first Detroit Conference of the St. Vincent de Paul Society, a charitable organization to assist the poor, was established at Ss. Peter and Paul Church in the mid-1880s. The St. Vincent de Paul Society Detroit organization's first president was parishioner Michael O'Brien, a benevolent banker represented in the framed photograph held by Patrick Adamcik, a 50-year staffer, in 2023 at the St. Vincent de Paul headquarters in Detroit. (Photograph by Patricia Montemurri.)

US representative Louis Rabaut attended Ss. Peter and Paul Elementary School and studied for his high school, college, and law school diplomas from the Jesuit-run Detroit College and its law school next door to the church. As a US congressman, he is credited with first introducing legislation to insert "under God" in the Pledge of Allegiance. He was a Democrat representing Detroit from 1935 to 1947 and 1949 until his death in 1961. A father to nine, he is pictured here with grandsons. His funeral Mass took place at Ss. Peter and Paul, where he had sung in the choir for decades. (Courtesy of the *Detroit Free Press*.)

Parishioner Thomas Chawke, second from right, worked with legendary attorney Clarence Darrow, far right, in pioneering civil rights cases. Darrow defended black physician Ossian Sweet, charged in a fatal shooting after an all-white mob threatened Dr. Sweet's home when he moved to an all-white neighborhood in 1925. The trial for Dr. Sweet ended in a hung jury. The doctor's brother Henry Sweet, far left, then went on trial for murder, and Chawke's defense of Henry Sweet convinced an all-white jury to acquit. The prosecutor decided not to retry Ossian Sweet and dismissed charges against others who had been inside the Sweet home when the mob attacked. Lawyer Julian Perry is pictured second from left. (Courtesy of the Walter P. Reuther Library, Wayne State University.)

The Reverend Arthur Lovely was a longtime associate pastor at Ss. Peter and Paul who created a ministry reaching out to inmates at the Wayne County Jail. He also worked with the Human Relations Club at the University of Detroit to encourage frank and honest discussions about race relations.

The Reverend Robert Hartigan (left) exemplified Ss. Peter and Paul's generosity to people experiencing homelessness or unemployment and dealing with the ravages of mental illness and substance abuse. In the winter of 1988, he began inviting people from the streets to seek refuge inside the church. That was the start of the parish's Warming Center, below, announced by the sign propped up on the church's front steps.

These photographs illustrate how the church's vestibule and hallways were used to provide shelter and warmth for homeless people escaping the winter cold. One gentleman (above) reclines in a pew placed in an alcove under historical parish photographs to sleep. Others drink coffee in chairs set up along the church's east hallway. (Both photographs by Mary Schroeder.)

In 2015, the Warming Center was renamed the Pope Francis Center to honor the first Jesuit priest to assume the papacy. With generous grants from the UAW-Ford fund and other sponsors, the church's St. Catherine Chapel at the rear of the church (left) was renovated to provide a gathering place, shower, laundry, and kitchen facilities to those in need. The parish continues a long tradition of service to the disadvantaged. The Pope Francis Center accepts donations to continue its vital work. To give via check, make the check payable to Pope Francis Center and mail it to 438 St. Antoine Street, Detroit, MI 48226. The Pope Francis Center also welcomes volunteers to help those experiencing homelessness. For more information, visit popefranciscenter.org, email the center at info@popefranciscenter. org, or call 313-964-2823. (Photograph by Visionalist Entertainment.)

Fr. Tim McCabe, a Jesuit priest, is the executive director of the Pope Francis Center, striving to eradicate chronic homelessness in Detroit. He has led a refugee settlement project in Detroit, served as the Midwest director of the Jesuit Volunteer Corps for 12 years, provided hospice support to San Francisco's homeless, directed development for Loyola High School Detroit, and spent two years with the Ignatian Spirituality Project coordinating retreats for homeless men and women. (Courtesy of the Pope Francis Center.)

Inside the Pope Francis Center, a variety of nourishment is provided in ways beyond food and beverage (above). Visitors can wash clothes, obtain essentials like socks and underwear, take showers, and seek help with problems from staffers and volunteers. The Pope Francis Center is open from 7:00 a.m. to 11:00 a.m. Monday through Saturday. (Photograph by Visionalist Entertainment.)

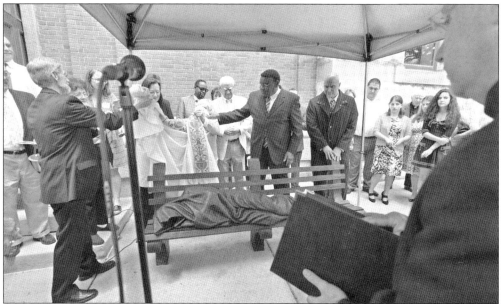

In a June 2015 ceremony, Ss. Peter and Paul Church installed a sculpture known as *Homeless Jesus*. The bronze sculpture features a life-size man lying on a seven-foot park bench. A blanket obscures most of the man's body, but the marks of Jesus's crucifixion are visible on his bare feet. At the dedication, the statue's creator, Ontario artist Timothy Schmalz, stands at the right end of the sculptured bench. Standing to the left of Schmalz is Detroit deputy mayor Isaiah McKinnon. (Photograph by Jessica Trevino.)

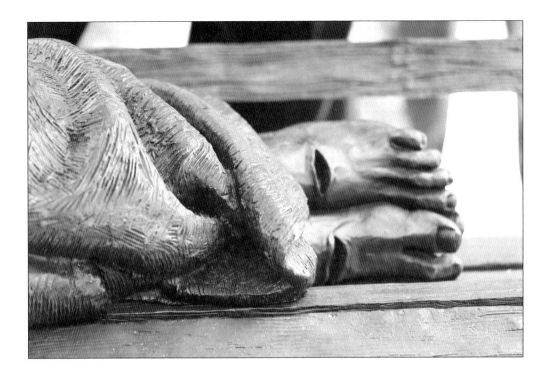

The above photograph showcases the element of *Homeless Jesus* many find most moving—the crucifixion wounds. Below, volunteers and guests at the dedication ceremony contemplate and congregate for a closer look. (Both photographs by Jessica Trevino.)

For the Pope Francis Center's annual service commemorating those who died while homeless, a ceremonial casket is prepared to be brought to the front of Ss. Peter and Paul Jesuit Church on December 21, 2022. Students from University of Detroit Jesuit High School serve as ceremonial pallbearers. (Photograph by Ryan Garza; courtesy of the *Detroit Free Press*.)

Laura Tonarelli (right) of Livonia speaks with Janelle Jackson (left) of Detroit following the service. The service included a reading of the names of people experiencing homelessness who died during 2022. (Photograph by Ryan Garza; courtesy of the *Detroit Free Press*.)

Pope Francis Center staff member Chris Leon places a candle in honor of a Detroiter whose name was announced during a service commemorating those who died while homeless during 2022. Photographs of those who passed are displayed on an altar. (Photograph by Ryan Garza; courtesy of the *Detroit Free Press*.)

On the steps of Ss. Peter and Paul Jesuit Church, Samuel Lewis sits with a photograph of his child's mother, Alanna Wilkins, who died in September 2022 while homeless. She was among those whose lives were commemorated during the annual service. (Photograph by Ryan Garza; courtesy of the *Detroit Free Press*.)

Six

TRANSITIONS

In the 1940s, Ss. Peter and Paul Church had been painted white in preparation for the 100th anniversary of its opening and dedication in 1848. Detroit reached its peak population of 1.8 million in the 1950 census. But the rise of suburbanization, racial struggles, white flight, and the decline of the automobile industry all contributed to a profound drop in Detroit's population over the next several decades. Downtown to the west of the church was a commercial district. Residential neighborhoods to the east were bulldozed for so-called urban renewal projects and a freeway. By the 1960s, the paint was peeling, and the parishioners who passed through the church's doors had dwindled substantially. Jesuit leaders seriously considered closing the church. (Courtesy of the *Detroit Free Press*.)

The photograph above captures the view of buildings along Jefferson Avenue as cars emerged from the Detroit-Windsor Tunnel, which snakes under the Detroit River to link the United States and Canada, in the early 1970s. Ss. Peter and Paul is visible in the upper center of the photograph. The large parking lot near the tunnel eventually would be unearthed for the mid-1970s construction of the Renaissance Center. The image below captures the church in 1964 during the construction of the I-375 freeway. (Above, courtesy of the Detroit Historical Society; below, courtesy of the *Detroit Free Press*.)

The late-1960s photograph, at right, captures a Sunday Mass as parishioners and Fr. Clement Singer, the church's pastor, fought against recommendations to close the historic church. Above is an aerial view of the church and the adjacent University of Detroit Law School, which once housed the high school and college programs known as Detroit College. Behind the church, the vacant convent of the Sisters of Charity nuns who taught at the grade school remained standing before eventual demolition. The Ss. Peter and Paul grade school had closed in 1964. Jesuit superiors wanted to close the church and make it a library for the law school. On February 13, 1972, parishioners gathered for what was to be the church's final Mass. Instead, Father Singer announced the Jesuits had reversed their decision, and the historic church would remain open. (Both, courtesy of the *Detroit Free Press*.)

This 1960s-era photograph captures Fr. Clement Singer (second from right), pastor of Ss. Peter and Paul, holding a piece of water piping from the 1820s unearthed from a street near the church as construction was underway for the Michigan Blue Cross Blue Shield insurance building. The water pipes in Detroit's early days were carved out of logs. Pictured with him are, from left to right, Rev. Ernest Blougouras of Annunciation Greek Orthodox Church, Fr. Alexander Bottazzo of Holy Family (Italian) Catholic Church, and Fr. John Nader of St. Mary Catholic Church in Greektown. Below is an undated interior view of a Mass at the church. (Above, photograph courtesy of the *Detroit Free Press*.)

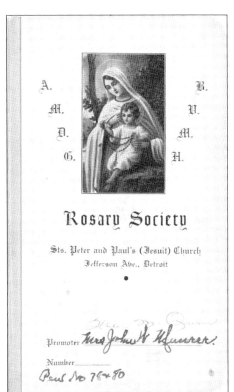

These two photographs point to how services and practices at church changed over the decades. At right is a Rosary Society booklet maintained by a parishioner that dates back to when pews could be assigned and reserved for families. Below is a photograph taken in 1979 when Wayne State University and its chorale group performed at the church along with dancers.

Construction on Detroit's Renaissance Center began in 1973, and the first of five towers was completed in 1976. Ss. Peter and Paul Church, visible on the far right, has stood steady as the landscape around it has constantly evolved since 1844. (Courtesy of the Detroit Historical Society.)

The Reverend Joseph Tobin (far right), the associate pastor of Ss. Peter and Paul, blessed the launching ceremony for canoeist Tony Lenzini (second from left), who sought to voyage from Detroit to Moscow in May 1979. Father Tobin led Ss. Peter and Paul in welcoming Filipino families, including many who worked as nurses at nearby hospitals, to the congregation. (Courtesy of the *Detroit Free Press*.)

Members of the parish's Filipino community harmonize for the Christmas Choir in 1980.

Fr. Robert Rosenfelder, a Jesuit priest, presides at a service at Ss. Peter and Paul in November 1989 to commemorate six Jesuit priests and two others who were brutally murdered at the University of Central America in El Salvador. Members of the Salvadoran military murdered them because they spoke out against a thuggish government and in support of the poor. (Courtesy of the *Detroit Free Press.*)

There is much to delight the eye at Ss. Peter and Paul Jesuit Church. In this 1970s-era photograph, a group studies the fine details of the church's altar, donated by the Fleitz family and carved from Italian Carrara marble.

This architectural sketch shows the design for a 1973 law library addition to the University of Detroit Mercy Law School, adjacent to Ss. Peter and Paul Church. The addition created a courtyard in the back of the campus between the church and the law school.

In 1959, the Jesuits opened a seminary in then rural Clarkston, some 40 miles from downtown Detroit. It was named Colombiere College after Jesuit missionary St. Claude Colombiere. The facility is now a complex for aging and infirm Jesuits. Part of the property was developed into a golf course, Shepherd's Hollow. Colombiere Center is also a retreat and conference center operated by the Midwest Province of the Society of Jesus. Pictured below is the center's chapel during a visit by Fr. Peter-Hans Kolvenbach, the Jesuit superior general, in 2006. (Above, courtesy of the Jesuit Archive & Research Center; below, courtesy of Michael Sarnacki.)

In 1993, the Jesuits founded a new all-boys high school in Detroit. The school's mission is to nurture "a culture of hope and academic success for young men challenged by an urban environment and prepares them to be men of Christian love, justice and service, who act with integrity, compassion and courage." It is housed in the former St. Francis de Sales Church and school (above) in northwest Detroit. The school features the innovative Loyola Work Experience Program, in which upper-class students spend one school day weekly at a job site, where they learn valuable skills and their salaries offset tuition costs. Below, the 2022 graduating class tosses caps high at Detroit's Cathedral of the Most Blessed Sacrament. (Above, photograph by Patricia Montemurri; below, courtesy of Loyola High School.)

Seven

TRADITIONS

Ss. Peter and Paul welcomes people of all faiths to visit the church. Such was the case on World Sabbath Day in January 2002. In the aftermath of the September 11, 2001, attacks on the United States, when terrorists crashed planes into buildings in God's name, the event was designed to bring people together. In Detroit, faith leaders from various denominations gathered at Ss. Peter and Paul for a service. Children from area schools led the way, carrying flowers and olive branches, which symbolize peace. As a worship site since 1848, Ss. Peter and Paul has hosted legions of people seeking spiritual sustenance and renewal. (Photograph by Hugh Grannum; courtesy of the *Detroit Free Press*.)

Carved out of the church's east altar is the ambry, a glass cabinet. Inside are the holy oils (above) priests use to anoint those seeking the sacraments of baptism, confirmation, and the anointing of the sick. Below, Fr. Ronald Torina (far left) baptized Erin Blackwell, cradled in her grandmother Mary Blackwell's arms, in 1997 at the church. Erin's parents, Bill and Kim Blackwell, stand behind Mary Blackwell. Father Torina taught the baby's father at University of Detroit Jesuit High School. (Courtesy of the Blackwell family.)

Edith Conroy is one happy baby as she is baptized into the Catholic faith by Fr. Gary Wright at Ss. Peter and Paul Jesuit in April 2023. Edith is held aloft by her mother, Mary Maloney. At left is Edith's father, Shane Conroy. At right are godmother Elizabeth Conroy and godfather Ryan Conroy. The parish has recorded more than 15,000 baptisms at the church's original wood-carved baptismal font since 1849. Among them is Akila Malaika Rwage, the daughter of Alain Jardin Rwage and Nancy Mukuri, pictured at right, who was baptized in 2022. Both Alain and Nancy are natives of Burundi. Alain proposed to Nancy after Mass one day. He told her he wanted to take a picture in front of the altar. "It begins with God. I knew I should do it the right way," Alain recounts. "Some go to the beach and have a lot of people around. We were with God. Jesus was around. Why not?" Nancy was surprised: "I wasn't aware at all what was happening. We went up front and then, he was at his knees. I smiled and laughed and, of course, I said Yes!" (Right, courtesy of the Rwage family.)

Some 7,000 couples have been married at Ss. Peter and Paul. In 1929, it hosted the wedding of Elizabeth Briggs, the daughter of Detroit Tigers baseball team owner Walter Briggs. She grew up on Boston Boulevard and married the boy next door, Charles Fisher Jr., the son of one of the original Fisher brothers who founded the Fisher Body division of automaker General Motors. Detroit's iconic Fisher Building also was constructed by the family. Charles Fisher Jr. attended University of Detroit, adjacent to the church. When he died in 1958, his funeral Mass was celebrated at Ss. Peter and Paul. (Left, courtesy of the Walter P. Reuther Library, Wayne State University; below, courtesy of the *Detroit Free Press*.)

Their vows made, Paul Diehl was allowed to kiss his bride, Patricia Montemurri, at the altar of Ss. Peter and Paul Church. The celebrant was the Reverend Luigi Maggioni (center), a priest with an Italian missionary order. The bride's sister Donna (Montemurri) Duffield is smiling at left. Paul Diehl's great-grandfather Charles P. Friederichs Jr., who is pictured on page 28, attended the original Jesuit-established Detroit College in 1882 and 1883. (Photograph by Tom Hagerty Photography.)

In 2010, Rhoda Henderson and Al Fields were married at the church by onetime pastor Fr. Carl Bonk. (Photograph by Modern Wedding Photography; courtesy of Rhoda Henderson Fields.)

The church has hosted multiple ordinations of Jesuit priests and brothers. On October 7, 2006, Brother John Moriconi (kneeling) professed his final vows. The Jesuit superior general, Fr. Peter Hans Kolvenbach (standing right), presided over the vows. Fr. Robert Scullin (standing left) and Fr. Carl Bonk, the church's pastor (behind the altar), witnessed the vows. (Photograph by Michael Sarnacki.)

The parish pastor, Fr. Robert Hartigan, welcomed Cardinal Adam Maida, who oversaw the six-county Archdiocese of Detroit from 1990 to 2009, as Ss. Peter and Paul celebrated its 150th anniversary. Hartigan was the founder of the parish's Warming Center and served as pastor from 1990 until his death at the age of 67 on Christmas Eve 1998.

Ss. Peter and Paul parishioners, joined by churchgoers at other nearby Catholic churches, gathered in a procession for the Feast of Corpus Christi in 2010. Included in the procession were sisters wearing the white and blue habits of the order founded by St. Mother Teresa of Calcutta.

In November 2017, to advance interfaith relations, Catholic leaders and officials from the Church of Jesus Christ of Latter-day Saints (LDS) hosted an Interfaith Religious Freedom Conference at Ss. Peter and Paul. Detroit archbishop Allen Vigneron was among the keynote speakers. He is pictured here with several faith leaders. (Photograph by Dave Frechette; courtesy of the Michigan Catholic Conference.)

The first Red Mass, a service for all those who serve in the legal profession, in a Catholic church in the United States was celebrated at Ss. Peter and Paul Church in 1877, during the first year that the Jesuits took over ownership of the building. In this 1930s photograph, law students and lawyers process from the University of Detroit Law School in Dowling Hall, adjacent to the church, through the main doors of Ss. Peter and Paul.

In this mid-1980s photograph, Detroit auxiliary bishop Moses Anderson exits a Red Mass at Ss. Peter and Paul as scores of black-robed judges file out behind him. The white-haired judge behind him is Michigan Supreme Court justice G. Mennen "Soapy" Williams, a onetime Michigan governor. To the left of Williams is Michigan Supreme Court justice James Brickley, a onetime Michigan lieutenant governor. In the center aisle farthest back at right is Michigan Appeals Court judge Roman Gribbs, Detroit mayor from 1969 to 1973. (Courtesy of the *Detroit Free Press*.)

Michigan Supreme Court justice G. Mennen "Soapy" Williams (far right) peruses the Red Mass program at a service at Ss. Peter and Paul Jesuit Church. To the left is Michigan Supreme Court justice James Ryan, who later became a US district judge. (Courtesy of the *Detroit Free Press*.)

As the Red Mass commences each year at Ss. Peter and Paul, it is tradition for law students at the adjacent University of Detroit Mercy Law School to process into the church with flags of the St. Thomas More Society. Sir Thomas More was a brilliant scholar and lawyer who served King Henry VIII until he was beheaded because he refused to approve the king's divorce of Catherine of Aragon to free Henry to marry Anne Boleyn. (Courtesy of the University of Detroit Mercy School of Law.)

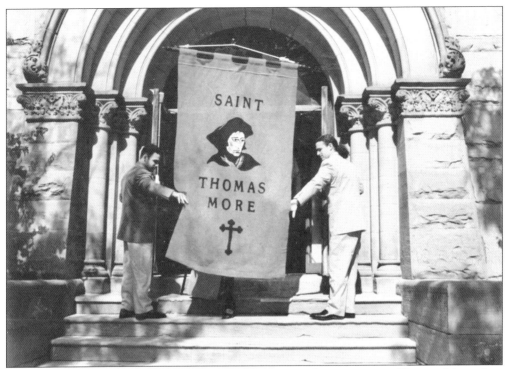

Another Red Mass procession begins for law students at the University of Detroit Mercy Law School's Dowling Hall entrance. (Courtesy of the University of Detroit Mercy School of Law.)

US district judge Terrence Berg (first row, left) and Michigan Appeals Court judge Michael Talbot (first row, third from left) raise their hands to take the Oath of Commitment. It states, in part: "I will never reject, from any consideration personal to myself, the cause of the defenseless or oppressed, or delay any cause for lucre or malice; I will in all other respects conduct myself personally and professionally in conformity with the high standards of conduct imposed upon members of the bar as conditions for the privilege to practice law in this State." (Courtesy of the Michigan Catholic.)

University of Detroit Mercy Law School dean Jelani Jefferson Exum is seen here at the 2022 Red Mass with arms outstretched. Standing next to her is Arnold D'Ambrosio, university vice president for advancement, and Pamela Zarkowski, provost and vice president for academic affairs of the University of Detroit Mercy. (Courtesy of the University of Detroit Mercy Law School.)

Msgr. John Zenz, pastor of Holy Name Church in Birmingham, celebrates the 2019 Red Mass at Ss. Peter and Paul. Mass-goers recite the St. Thomas More oath: "Lord, grant that I may be able in argument, accurate in analysis, strict in study, candid with clients, and honest with adversaries. Sit with me at my desk and listen with me to my client's plaints, read with me in the library, and stand beside me in court, so that today I shall not, in order to win a point, lose my soul." (Courtesy of the University of Detroit Mercy Law School.)

As it has for much of its history, Ss. Peter and Paul Church hosts Baccalaureate Masses for graduates of the Jesuit-founded professional schools, whose graduates excel as lawyers and dentists. The 2018 Baccalaureate Mass for the University of Detroit Mercy School of Law was held at the church. Above, graduates process in against the backdrop of Detroit's Renaissance Center. Inside, a graduate partakes from the chalice holding the consecrated wine during communion. (Both, courtesy of the University of Detroit Mercy Law School.)

Eight

THE PEOPLE
OF GOD TODAY

On Easter Sunday 2022, the Reverend Gary Wright showers the congregation with the Gospel's good news and holy water. Pastor since 2015, he is shepherding the congregation through its 175th anniversary since the church opened in 1848. He entered the Jesuits in 1967. He also has served as a campus minister at the University of Detroit Mercy and has led Faith in the D gatherings, where young people meet to discuss topics about commitment and spirituality. More and more young people are taking up residence in the city in onetime office buildings and stores converted into apartments and condos. One of Father Wright's goals is to make Ss. Peter and Paul "a center of young adult spirituality and community in the heart of the rebirth of downtown Detroit." (Photograph by Diane Weiss.)

One sign of Detroit's renaissance is increased interest in its history. The Detroit Mass Mob movement was launched in 2014 to bring attention to landmark churches in the city, some struggling with finances and lack of parishioners. The Detroit Mass Mob, reaching out through mainstream and social media, asked curious Catholics to fill the pews at a historic church once a month. Mass Mob attendees enjoy seeing the city churches, some so ornate as to rival European cathedrals. On November 8, 2015, it was Ss. Peter and Paul's turn to show off the oldest church in Detroit. Pictured from left to right below are parishioners Richard Pasiak, Jamie Cicchelli, Donna Versele, and Michael Solner. (Both, courtesy of Michael Sarnacki.)

Detroit deputy mayor Isaiah McKinnon (right) attended the Mass Mob service. Next to him is his son Jason McKinnon, who is standing next to his mother and Isaiah McKinnon's wife, Patrice McKinnon. (Courtesy of Michael Sarnacki.)

The year 2015 marked the end of the Reverend Patrick Peppard's tenure as Ss. Peter and Paul administrator. He is seen here chatting with parishioner Antoinette Pasiak at the Mass Mob event. He also taught theology for years at the University of Detroit Jesuit High School. As a parish priest at St. Clement Church in Romeo in Macomb County, he served Mass alongside an altar boy named Robert Ritchie, now known as Kid Rock. (Courtesy of Michael Sarnacki.)

Ss. Peter and Paul pastor Fr. Gary Wright is the founder and Jesuit liaison for the Jesuit Friends and Alumni Network (JFAN) of Detroit. JFAN holds periodic luncheons featuring speakers with ties to the Jesuits. In Spring 2021, former University of Michigan basketball coach John Beilein (left), who was educated by Jesuits at Wheeling University in West Virginia, spoke to JFAN Detroit. To his right is William Duffield, a University of Detroit Jesuit High School graduate and then University of Detroit Mercy Law School student. To learn more about JFAN, visit www.jfanusa.org/detroit. (Photograph by Donna Duffield.)

Nettie Seabrooks is a Ss. Peter and Paul parishioner who has attended the church for several decades. She broke through glass ceilings when she served in the administration of Detroit mayor Dennis Archer in the early 2000s. She was the first woman to serve as a mayoral chief of staff and chief operating officer and also served as Archer's deputy mayor. (Courtesy of the *Detroit Free Press*.)

This sculpture draws the eye in its location outside the courtyard door to Ss. Peter and Paul Church. It represents a vision that St. Ignatius of Loyola experienced on his way to Rome just prior to the founding of the Jesuit order. According to his autobiography and the testimony of his companions, he saw God the Father commend him (Ignatius) to serve Jesus carrying His cross, in a way that profoundly confirmed the founding and naming of the new order, the Society of Jesus. (Photograph by Mary Schroeder.)

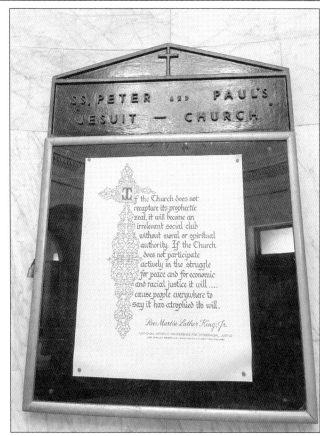

In the vestibule of Ss. Peter and Paul Church is this reminder of the words of slain civil rights leader Rev. Martin Luther King Jr. (Photograph by Visionalist Entertainment.)

For several years in a row, Ss. Peter and Paul Jesuit Church has hosted a Mass on the Saturday night before the Detroit Free Press International Marathon dedicated to ministering to runners. It is called "The Blessing of the Sneakers." The sanctuary is decorated with running gear and marathon medals. Fr. Gary Wright wears running shoes as he celebrates Mass. At left, Rebecca Adewumi of Hoffman Estates, Illinois, came to Detroit to run her first half-marathon in 2022. "I feel like prayer always helps," she said. Below, runners carry their shoes with them for a blessing. (Both photographs by Patricia Montemurri.)

Ss. Peter and Paul Jesuit Church and several staff members were featured in a PBS/Detroit Public Television documentary about historic Detroit places of worship. The film, *Detroit: The City of Churches*, also highlighted the work of the Pope Francis Center under its director, the Reverend Timothy McCabe. Above is the marquee of Detroit's Fillmore Theatre when the film had a big-screen premiere on December 10, 2022, before it was broadcast on Detroit Public Television. Below, filmmaker Keith Famie interviews Fr. Gary Wright in the historic church. (Above, photograph by Patricia Montemurri; below, photograph by Visionalist Entertainment.)

Many parishioners are eager for community activities to help others. Above, parishioners gathered on Detroit's Belle Isle to help with clean-up in 2019. Below, the parish's Contemplative Leaders in Action (CLA) program organizes Christmas gift wrapping and gift giving for children of families served by It's Life Remodeled, a Detroit neighborhood nonprofit. To learn more about CLA, visit www.contemplativeleaders.org/detroit. (Above, photograph by Junfu Han.)

Archbishop Allen Vigneron ordered a reorganization of Detroit Catholic parishes to share resources, programs, and priests in light of the dwindling number of priests. In the Family of Parishes reorganization, Ss. Peter and Paul will work with Gesu Parish, a natural pairing since Gesu was founded by the Jesuits in 1922. Auxiliary Bishop Donald Hanchon, center, celebrated the new arrangement in an October 13, 2022, Mass at Gesu as children from Ss. Peter and Paul parish present the bread and wine.

Gesu Parish celebrated the 100th anniversary of its founding with a reunion that drew 1,000 current and former parishioners and scores of school alumni in July 2022. Those gathered included, from left to right, the following: Jesuit priests Fathers Gerald Cavanagh, Bernie Owens, Patrick Kelly, Gilbert Sunghera, and Jeff Dorr; Detroit auxiliary bishop Donald Hanchon, Jesuit Fathers Lorn Snow, Mark George, and Gary Wright; Deacon Gene Leger; and Jesuit Father Innocent Kamanzi. (Courtesy of the Gesu Catholic Parish.)

Fr. Gary Wright (far left) thanked and blessed Ss. Peter and Paul parish council members for their work in October 2022 as their terms came to an end with the Family of Parishes reorganization. The outgoing members are, from left to right, Joanne Petz, Donna Ridella, Rhoda Henderson, Tom Schuelke, Boratha Tan, and Korin Visocchi. (Chair Amy Amador not pictured.)

The Ss. Peter and Paul Parish support team gathers for the weekly Wednesday afternoon meeting. From left to right around the table are Rebecca McMaster, director of parish life; volunteer Susan Solner; Fr. Gary Wright; volunteer Donna Ridella; music and liturgy director Julie Berra; and director of operations Lydia Maola.

Ss. Peter and Paul was the setting for musical quartets performing in the candlelight concert program called "From Bach to the Beatles" against the dramatic backdrop of the church illuminated by hundreds of flameless candles in December 2022. (Photograph by Tom Hagerty Photography.)

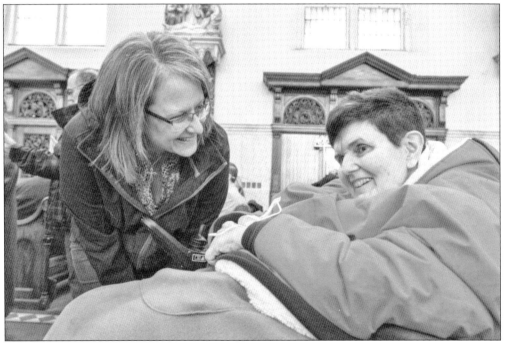

Lydia Maola (left), director of operations at Ss. Peter and Paul, greets parishioner Mary Schroeder (right) at Easter Mass in April 2022. Mary Schroeder was a longtime *Detroit Free Press* photographer, and she took the iconic photograph of Detroit Tigers player Kirk Gibson jumping in the air after hitting the three-run homer that won the 1984 World Series. She photographed many of the images in this book. (Photograph by Diane Weiss.)

With their wedding in June 2023, Amanda Pierzynski and Peter Phillips became the 7,000th couple to be married at Ss. Peter and Paul. It was important for them to have their wedding in downtown Detroit. They enjoy the city and its sporting events, sharing lunch downtown near Amanda's law office and coming to Mass at the church. "I didn't just want to register because of the wedding," Peter said of becoming Ss. Peter and Paul parishioners. "I wanted to join a parish that was doing good work in the city. Something I could share with my kids one day." (Photograph by Taylor Marie Parker.)

It has been several years since Ss. Peter and Paul Church celebrated the First Communion of a young parishioner. In evidence of a growing number of young families joining the parish, Peach Scheulke made her First Communion at the church on May 14, 2023. Her parents, Tom and Kristy Scheulke, stand alongside her as Fr. Gary Wright offers her the Holy Eucharist. (Photograph by Debbie Miszak.)

A mini-orchestra often fills the church with inspirational music. Above, the orchestra and choir, with trumpeter Bill Cable center, perform during Easter Mass 2023. The Ss. Peter and Paul musicians and choirs are led by Julie Berra, seated at the piano below, during Easter Mass 2022. Since Pentecost 2016, she has been the director of music and liturgy. The parish's music is a unique blend of traditional, folk, and contemporary styles, led by a vocal choir and a mix of instruments, including organ, piano, guitar, wind and string instruments, and drums. The musicians are volunteers from within the parish community who are drawn not only by the joy of making music together, but also the deep sense of community and fellowship. (Above; photograph by Patricia Montemurri; below, photograph by Diane Weiss.)

During Easter Mass 2022 (above), which marks Jesus's resurrection from the dead, Fr. Gary Wright recites the Eucharistic Prayer. It is the heart of the Mass celebration and is when Catholics believe the bread and the wine become the body and blood of Jesus Christ. Below, parishioner Cindy Brady receives communion from parish Eucharistic minister Marsha Salley. (Both photographs by Diane Weiss.)

Parishioners keep their children occupied during Easter Mass in April 2022 in an area of the nave dubbed the "The Prayground," created from a former confessional. Families with children, such as Catherine Martin and her daughter Madeleine Martin at far right, know they are welcome here. (Photograph by Diane Weiss.)

Barbara Beauregard (far left) and her parents, Margaret and William Beauregard, join hands as they recite the Our Father prayer during Easter Mass in 2022. (Photograph by Diane Weiss.)

After a Sunday Mass in December 2022, Ss. Peter and Paul parishioners gathered for the church's annual Christmas party potluck. They used the Atrium gathering space in the University of Detroit Mercy Law School, across a courtyard separating the back of the church from the school. In 2023, the parish is celebrating 175 years since it first opened its door. Today, many of its parishioners are from the suburbs, and about half are Detroiters who live downtown or nearby in neighborhoods such as Lafayette Park and Midtown. "God has been busy planting seeds of new life among us—some have already sprouted, a few are in full bloom, and some are still germinating, waiting for their time to come," Fr. Gary Wright wrote parishioners. "We average one new household registration

nearly every week. Babies have been born to our younger parishioners. Babies have grown and we now have started a children's liturgy program," according to the parish website. "We cannot help but be joyfully grateful for all this new life. Yet more is on the way: a thousand new housing units will be built in our parish area in the next few years. So, we must also be on our knees in earnest prayer that, as a community, we can rise to what this new life requires of us: that we can engage enough people and resources to provide the ministry and spiritual nourishment that people need in order to find a spiritual home here, and to continue bringing the welcoming Light of Christ into the heart of the city." (Photograph by Tom Hagerty Photography.)

There is a wide selection of sweet and savory goodies at the buffet table for the parish Christmas party above. Below, parishioners Jack and Sarah Walsworth light up because of the festivities. (Both photographs by Tom Hagerty Photography.)

Above, brothers Orlando (left) and Santino (right) Visocchi are all heart with their candy canes in hand. Below, Hollie Webb and her daughter get a table-side visit from Santa, also known as parishioner Marty Petz. (Both photographs by Tom Hagerty Photography.)

Above, this table is thinking merry thoughts. From left to right are Jeremy Alexander, Toni Boger, Sarah MacMaster, Debbie Miszak, and Rebecca MacMaster. Below, Joanne Dula delights in the day. (Both photographs by Tom Hagerty Photography.)

Ss. Peter and Paul Jesuit Church was placed in the National Register of Historic Places in 1971. This historical marker from the State of Michigan recaps its legacy as the oldest church building in Detroit and notes that the structure retains "its original simplicity and dignity." (Photograph by Tom Hagerty Photography.)

There are small treasures in every corner of this church. A glass case in the church's side hallway displayed reliquaries holding relics from the remains of Catholic saints. (Photograph by Tom Hagerty Photography.)

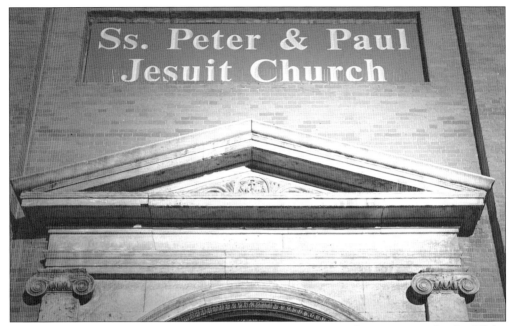

In preparation for the 175th anniversary in 2023, the church's name was once again affixed to the front of the church above the main door. For many of its years in existence, the church's name was not prominently displayed on its exterior. New ironwork railings bearing the Jesuit seal were installed on the church's front steps to provide support to all who enter and exit, including for Easter Sunday 2023 worshippers at left. (Above, photograph by Tom Hagerty Photography; left, photograph by Patricia Montemurri.)

Bridging three different centuries and at the corner of St. Antoine Street and Jefferson Avenue since its cornerstone was laid in 1844, Ss. Peter and Paul today strives to welcome spiritual seekers. Its website issues this invitation: "Reflecting the welcome that Jesus Christ offers to all, Ss. Peter and Paul Parish welcomes every person to seek full participation in our parish community without regard to age, sex, race, cultural background, physical or mental health or ability, sexual orientation, gender identity, social or economic situation, marital status, or faith background." (Photograph by Tom Hagerty Photography.)

175TH ANNIVERSARY

Ss. PETER & PAUL
JESUIT CHURCH
1848-2023

A WELCOMING
CHRISTIAN COMMUNITY
IN THE HEART OF
DETROIT

With this banner announcing its 175th anniversary celebration in 2023, Ss. Peter and Paul stands as a bedrock beacon of faith in the landscape of Detroit. "We do not seek to erase our differences," its website proclaims, "but rather lovingly embrace the uniqueness of each person as we strive to grow together in holiness."

Under a bright sun and blue skies, Ss. Peter and Paul parishioners gathered on the church steps after Easter Day Mass 2023. Parishioners and staff are committed to the continuing revival of the city of Detroit and the parish's vital and evolving role, with Jesuit pastors at its helm. "Telling the story of Ss. Peter and Paul's past has made me more in awe than ever of the great people on whose shoulders we stand, and the great legacy we've inherited," says Fr. Gary Wright, its pastor. "But perhaps even more awesome is the potential we have now as a young and growing presence in downtown Detroit. We are living witnesses that faith in Christ and our Jesuit spirituality still bring forth new life and enable us to be a welcoming presence for all who come, and still empower us to offer ourselves in service to others." (Photograph by Patricia Montemurri.)

About the Organization

Ss. Peter and Paul Jesuit Church is alive and thriving today. It is the spiritual home for people who live in or near Detroit's resurgent downtown as well as those who work in surrounding office buildings. Its parishioners come from 83 different zip codes all over metropolitan Detroit.

Many people who are alumni of Jesuit schools seek out a Jesuit parish to sustain them in their adult lives. Others are drawn to parishes run by Jesuit priests because of the quality of preaching, or the parish's sense of hospitality and welcome in its liturgies, or its commitment to the service of others. Ss. Peter and Paul parish today continues a long tradition of service to the disadvantaged. Currently, a task force is actively searching out new service commitments. It remains home to the Pope Francis Center, which provides basic services to about 200 people experiencing homelessness. The center accepts donations and also welcomes volunteers. See www.popefranciscenter.org for more information.

As more and more college graduates and young job seekers gravitate to living in downtown Detroit, the parish has provided programs targeted to their spiritual journeys. These include Faith in the D, which meets regularly at local watering holes for socializing and spirituality discussions.

The parish also sponsors Contemplative Leaders in Action (CLA), a national program for young adults flourishing in 10 cities. It helps young professionals integrate their spiritual life and values into their workplace, family, and community. A leadership development program based on principles of Ignatian spirituality, CLA builds on the teachings of St. Ignatius Loyola, the founder of the Jesuit order of priests and brothers who continue to steer the parish. To learn more about CLA, visit www.contemplativeleaders.org/detroit.

The parish's current frontier is developing children's and family programming for the many youthful faces that now fill the pews. To learn more about Ss. Peter and Paul parish, visit ssppjesuit.org, call 313-961-8077, or email office@ssppjesuit.org. The parish's mailing address is 438 St. Antoine Street, Detroit, MI 48226.

Discover Thousands of Local History Books
Featuring Millions of Vintage Images

Arcadia Publishing, the leading local history publisher in the United States, is committed to making history accessible and meaningful through publishing books that celebrate and preserve the heritage of America's people and places.

Find more books like this at
www.arcadiapublishing.com

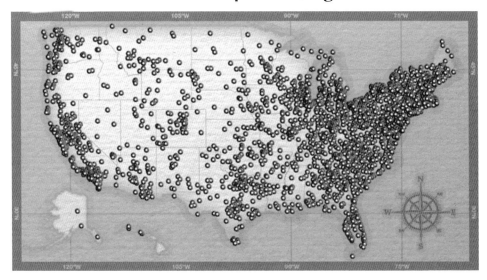

Search for your hometown history, your old stomping grounds, and even your favorite sports team.

Consistent with our mission to preserve history on a local level, this book was printed in South Carolina on American-made paper and manufactured entirely in the United States. Products carrying the accredited Forest Stewardship Council (FSC) label are printed on 100 percent FSC-certified paper.

MADE IN THE USA